GW00457567

Courchevel & the 3 Valleys

A Mad Dog Ski resort guide

Second edition 2008
Published by Mad Dog Ski
maddogski.com

Mad Dog Ski
Courchevel & the 3 Valleys
Second edition 2008

Published by Mad Dog Ski
Maps © Mad Dog Ski

Edited by: Kim Davidson, Kate Whittaker
Design: David Marshall
Artwork: Paddi Graphics
Printed by: Etrinsic

ISBN 978-0-9551215-0-0

A catalogue record of this book is available at the British Library.

Mad Dog Ski, PO Box 6321, Bournemouth, BH1 9ED, UK
info@maddogski.com
maddogski.com
+44 (0) 845 054 2906

To Alex & Jo
'Enjoy your time in Courchevel' 2010/11
Love
Mum & Dad
_xx_

Contents

About Mad Dog Ski

About Courchevel

Planning your trip

On the piste

Food and drink

Other things to do

Children

The list

Maps

About Mad Dog Ski resort guides and why we hope they'll make a real difference to your holiday.

About Mad Dog Ski

My time in the mountains used to be restricted to one or two precious weeks a year. Each winter, I would arrive with my ski buddies, eager to get on the slopes as soon as possible, indulge in some good après-ski and ensure we had somewhere decent to re-fuel at lunchtimes. All too often, these are things you discover the day before you're heading home.

During my first season as a thirty-something chalet host, I realised I wasn't alone in my quest for reliable information. Week after week guests would ask the same questions; where should they ski, where were the best places to eat and drink, the best mountain restaurants (and how do you get there)? Mad Dog Ski was born.

Everything in our books and on maddogski.com is researched by skiers and boarders who know the resort they are writing about inside out.

Our researchers are passionate about helping you get the most out of your holiday from the moment you arrive to the moment you leave. We want you to love the resort as much as we do.

With Mad Dog Ski, you'll always get our independent view – extra special places and people are shown as 'Mad Dog favourites'. If you find places we haven't, please write to us or email us at **info@maddogski.com.**

Enjoy the mountain!

Kate Whittaker
Founder, Mad Dog Ski

About this book

This book is designed to be most useful when you actually get to Courchevel. To keep it small enough to fit in your jacket pocket, we have put most of the planning information on **maddogski.com** (travel options, where to stay and other important stuff). Email us with any questions for which you cannot find an answer – we love a challenge!

We're not perfect!

Whilst we make every effort to get things right, places, prices and opening times do change from season to season. If you spot an error or if you simply have a different opinion to us, please let us know at info@maddogski.com.

Prices

All prices are based on the 2006/7 season and are given in (€) euro.

Skier or boarder?

Throughout this book, 'skiing' and 'skier' are used as interchangeable terms for 'riding' and 'boarder'. No offence intended – it just seems easier that way.

Telephone numbers

All numbers are prefixed by their French international dialling code – 00 33 (referred to as +33 throughout this book). French mobile numbers always start with '6'.

Dialling from the UK to France – drop the first '0' of the French number. For example when phoning (0)4 79 08 40 40,

dial 00 33 4 79 08 40 40. From France to the UK, dial '00 44' and drop the first '0' of the UK area code.

You'll find public telephones that accept phone cards available throughout the resort. Buy your phone card from a tabac.

If you plan to use your UK mobile in Courchevel, you should check with your network provider that it is activated for international calls before leaving the UK. You pay to receive calls as well as make them, so text messages are often a cheaper way to stay in touch.

Tell us what you think!

Tell us about your favourite (or least favourite) places in Courchevel at maddogski.com. Simply check out the entry under our 'Mad Dog listings' section and click 'Write review' or 'Rating'.

We'd love to hear from you; you can contact us by email, post or through our website. Our contact details are given at the front of this book.

About our researchers

Sheryl Davies

After a year of travelling around France and Spain in a VW Campervan, Sheryl stumbled into the French Alps. The lifestyle that comes with living in and around Courchevel soon became addictive and Sheryl has now spent four winter seasons working in resort.

Her spare time is spent on the mountains skiing or hiking the numerous walking trails.

Favourite restaurant: L'Oeil de Boeuf, 1550
Best après-ski: Les Peupliers, Le Praz
Favourite mountain restaurant: Le Roc Tania, Courchevel
Best piste: Combe Saulire

About Mad Dog Ski

Home
Guidebooks
Features
News
Ski weekends
Gallery
Get in touch

Resorts
Austria
France
Switzerland

Courchevel - France

Anyone who has skied in Courchevel will usually mention two things; the skiing is superb but it comes at a price. Whilst the skiing is undeniably worth every euro, it is possible to ski here without taking out a second mortgage. It is both a resort where you can charter a private jet to fly into the tiny altiport and lunch at a two Michelin star restaurant; or you can arrive by coach and lunch on a €5 kebab (on the piste as well!).

There are five villages in Courchevel; 1850, 1650, 1550, Le Praz and La Tania. The villages descend in size as you go down the mountain and all have their own distinct feel. Whilst 1850 is perhaps more sophisticated, you will find a good choice of restaurants and bars in all the villages. Courchevel isn't a particularly cheap resort either, but there are budget options to be found further down the resort, especially in Le Praz. The shuttle bus links between the resorts is very good as well, so if you need to start your day in 1850 but are staying in another village, it will not take long to travel there.

Many visitors never bother leaving the village they are staying in all holiday, particularly those staying in a chalet. This is a shame as the villages all have something to offer and getting around is quite easy.

Courchevel & the 3 Valleys guidebook
Buy now

More...
Planning your trip
Where to stay
On the piste
Food and drink
Other activities
Families
The list
Webcams and weather

Snow reports
Courchevel

3

Courchevel; great skiing, glamour and an abundance of après-ski combine to make this resort totally unforgettable.

What you'll find in this chapter

Courchevel has always had a well-deserved reputation as one of the best resorts in the world, with a wide choice of slopes from challenging blacks and off-piste to long, gentle greens and cruisy blues.

Courchevel also has a reputation for being expensive but this is less deserved. Whilst you can definitely live the high life here (in every sense), you can also have a great holiday here on a relatively modest budget and the experience will be worth every penny.

Forming part of the Three Valleys, Courchevel is home to five villages, three of which are simply known by their altitude; 1850, 1650, 1550, La Tania (1350m) and the lowest village Le Praz (1300m) (shown opposite). Each village has easy lift access to the vast ski domain and has their own shops, restaurants and bars.

Courchevel's villages (more village maps are on page 155)

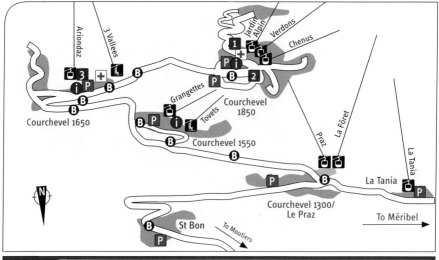

Key:

- **ⓘ** Tourist office
- **✚** Medical centre
- **Ⓑ** Ski bus stops

1. La Croisette
2. Le Forum
3. Maison du Moriond

Getting around: 1850's main landmarks and areas

- **La Croisette:** the central building in 1850 where you'll find the Jardin Alpin, Verdons and Chenus gondolas and ESF (French ski school)
- **Rue de Tovets:** the road running past the medical centre and down towards 1650, 1550, Le Praz and La Tania
- **Tourist office:** situated on Rue de Rocher

1850

1850 is the highest, largest village and home to most of the more expensive hotels and bars. Centred around La Croisette, it stretches out on either side making much of the accommodation ski in, ski out. Three long green pistes run back into resort, making it an ideal base for beginners.

1650

The next largest village after 1850, 1650 sits on a ridge with views across to 1850 and 1550. With great beginner slopes, this is an excellent resort for families and is well connected to 1850 via a regular shuttle bus.

1550

Located directly below 1850, the quickest route up for skiers and pedestrians is the gondola, which takes less than 10 minutes. Although 1550 has a more limited restaurant and bar choice than 1850 and 1650, this tends to be reflected in slightly cheaper prices.

La Tania
(Courchevel 1350m)

Purpose built for the 1992 Olympics, La Tania's central cluster of ugly apartment blocks is now surrounded by a host of charming wooden chalets stretching up the hill. Its proximity to Méribel makes it a great base from which to explore the Three Valleys.

Le Praz
(Courchevel 1300m)

With its Olympic standard ski jump and small lake, Le Praz is the lowest village in Courchevel. That said, its two lifts connect you easily with 1850 or Méribel and thanks to good snow cannons you can ski back to resort pretty much all season. This is the prettiest and smallest of the resorts and many residents live here all year round.

Ski area overview

The Three Valleys has some of the most extensive and impressive skiing in the world. Courchevel's pistes are primarily north-facing so the snow tends to last longer than its sunnier neighbour Méribel. For more on the skiing (> 21).

Courchevel at a glance

- Access to 600km of marked and interconnecting pistes

- 50% of slopes for beginners and intermediates, 50% for advanced and expert skiers

- 63 ski lifts (not including the Three Valleys system)

- 563 snow canons – 1,662 in the Three Valleys

- 22 piste bashers – 76 in the Three Valleys

- Runs from 3000m to 1300m

- More than 10,000 hectares off-piste

- Forests at over 2000m

- Over 60 restaurants

Don't leave Courchevel without...

- Arriving in style – fly in to Courchevel Altiport; €1450 for five people from Geneva (➤ 120)

- Taking the kids bowling (or just you!) in 1850 (➤ 119)

- Dining in style at the 2 Michelin star Chabichou hotel (➤ 82)

- Travelling to all three valleys in one day (➤ 59)

- Putting pedal to the metal on an ice circuit (➤ 123)

- Go-karting on ice for a real thrill (➤ 120)

- Indulging in the famous seafood platter at Le Cap Horn (➤ 106)

- Treating yourself to a massage at your chalet (➤ 119)

Helping you to
plan your trip;
your travel options,
where to stay and other
useful information.

Our books are designed to be a handy companion in resort. To keep them pocket sized, we try to keep the planning information and tips on our website **maddogski.com** (which also helps us to be as up-to-date as possible). This chapter gives you a simple overview together with useful websites and contacts.

maddogski.com

- Travel advice, including details for arriving in France (self-drive, trains, airlines and ferries) and how to get to resort once you arrive (airport transfer companies, car hire and buses)

- Accommodation, including reviews of chalets, hotels and apartments

- Everything else you need to know before you book your trip from winter sports insurance to the latest snow reports

Getting to Courchevel

If you're arranging your own travel (rather than booking a package holiday) you have several options. You can fly to Geneva, Lyon St Exupéry, Grenoble and Chambéry airports. Chambéry and Grenoble are closer but Geneva has the best track record of staying open in bad weather.

Remember to check ski and board baggage charges which can significantly push up the price of a 'cheap' flight. For up-to-date baggage information, check out **maddogski.com.**

The snow trains run by Eurostar and Rail Europe are a more eco-friendly route to the Alps with Eurostar carbon neutral from 2007. Eurostar runs direct services to Moûtiers from St Pancras or Ashford taking around eight hours. Choose an overnight train on Friday or Saturday, or daytime on Saturday. Although pricier (from £220) than low-cost airlines, the journey is relaxing, and you avoid lengthy transfers.

For a livelier experience, start your holiday early with Rail Europe's infamous party snow train from Calais (it involves a ferry from Dover).

For overnight travellers, it's unlikely your accommodation will be ready when you arrive, so you'll need to arrange somewhere to store your bags while you get on the slopes.

Regular buses run from Geneva airport (from €150 round trip) and Moûtiers train station (from €24). Whilst there are transfer links from other airports, these can be inconsistent and often mean lengthy waits at the airport so car hire or private transfers are the best options.

If you hire a car, remember to factor in car parking fees (around €70 for seven days), unless you're staying in Le Praz or La Tania which have free (uncovered) car parks. You are required by law to carry snow chains (you'll need to request these when you book).

For a door-to-door service, the English-speaking private transfer companies or taxis are a good

fast track to courchevel with the snow train

Why not take the Rail Europe's Snow Train? Depart Friday night from either St Pancras or Ebbsfleet International on Eurostar and connect with the overnight service in Paris. You'll arrive fresh for a full day of skiing on Saturday morning. Return the following Saturday night.

- Enjoy 2 extra days on the slopes!
- Comfortable, flat-bed sleeping accommodation
- Stops at 6 stations serving 25 resorts
- Bar and disco carriages
- Skis and snowboards go free
- Short, easy transfers to resort
- Bi-lingual reps on board

to Paris

Combloux
Megève
La Giettaz
Flumet   Praz-sur-Arly
Crest-Voland   N.D-de-Bellecombe
Les Saisies

La Féclaz
Albertville   Bourg   La Rosière
St Maurice   Val d'Isère
Les Allions   Arêches
Aime   Landry
Les Arcs   Tignes
Peisey-Vallandry
Chambéry   Moûtiers   La Plagne
Champagny-en-Vanoise
Courchevel
Key   Valmorel   La Tania   Pralognan
○ Train Station   Les Menuires   Méribel
● Ski Resort
Val Thorens

return from

£219

for Courchevel
take the
Snow Train
to Moûtiers

for more information and to book
call **0844 848 4062** or visit www.raileurope.co.uk

RAIL EUROPE

option (especially for early morning flights). They're not necessarily more expensive, particularly for larger groups (➤ 18).

If you're planning on driving from the UK, it should take around 12 hours to reach the Three Valleys once you arrive at your French port. French motorways are a lot emptier than the UK, although expect to pay between €50-60 in toll fees, either in cash or on credit card (not debit card).

Remember as well that the final approaches to resort can see huge tailbacks and delays in high season.

Airport transfer times

Airport	Airlines	km to Courchevel	Approx. transfer time by road
Chambéry	Flybe, Flyglobespan, Jet2	110km	1.5 hours
Geneva	Air France, bmi baby, BA, easyJet, Flybe, Flyglobespan, Jet 2, Swiss Air	150km	2.5 hours
Grenoble	BA, easyJet, Ryanair, Thomsonfly	127km	2 hours
Lyon St Exupéry	Air France, bmi baby, BA, easyJet	187km	2.5 hours

Where to stay

With everything from 4-star luxe hotels (France's equivalent to 5-star) to hostels, catered chalets to apartments, you should be able to find something to match your budget. You can get cheap last minute deals though these are rare in high season.

Check where your accommodation is before booking and also whether they offer a shuttle service to and from the slopes.

About Courchevel

> 7 for more about the different villages of Courchevel.

1850 offers the best choice for the hedonist. **Le Chabichou** (chabichou-courchevel.com) and **Hotel Les Grandes Alps**

are the most central. There's a wider choice slightly further from the centre and all the hotels run shuttle bus services. Don't forget luxury chalets from companies such as **Scott Dunn** (scottdunn.com).

For mid-priced hotels **Le Courcheneige** (courcheneige. com) is conveniently located right on the piste offering half-board accommodation and **Hotel Tovets** (courchevelhoteltovets.com) by La Croisette in 1850 is another good all-rounder.

Each of the other villages have hotel options too; notably the boutique **Seizena** (hotelseizena. com) in 1650, the very reasonably priced **Chalet Chanrossa** in 1550,

the **Hotel Telemark** (hoteltelemark.com) in La Tania and the long-standing favourite, **Les Peupliers** (lespeupliers.com) in Le Praz.

Catered chalets come in all sizes, but tend to sleep around 10 – 16 people. If your group isn't big enough to fill one, you'll end up sharing (and making new friends!). **maddogski.com** has a full list of all our favourites.

Self-caterers can choose between chalets or, more commonly, apartments. If you're too tired to cook after a day on the slops, try **>** 73 take-aways or **>** 74 restaurants.

Useful numbers and websites

Airports

Chambéry
T +33 (0)4 79 54 43 54
W chambery.aeroport.fr

Grenoble
T +33 (0)4 76 65 48 48
W grenoble.aeroport.fr

Geneva
T +41 (0)22 717 71 11
W gva.ch

Lyon St Exupéry
T +33 (0)4 26 00 70 07
W lyonairport.com

Airlines

Air France
T +44 (0)870 142 4343
W airfrance.co.uk

British Airways
T +44 (0)870 850 9850
W britishairways.com

bmi baby
T +44 (0)871 224 0224
W bmibaby.com

easyJet
T +44 (0)871 244 2366
W easyjet.com

Flybe
T +44 (0)871 522 6100
W flybe.com

Flyglobespan
T +44 (0)871 271 0415
W flyglobespan.com

Jet2
T +44 (0)871 226 1737
W jet2.com

Ryanair
T +44 (0)871 246 0000
W ryanair.com

Swiss
T +44 (0)845 601 0956
W swiss.com

Thomsonfly
T +44 (0)870 165 0079
W thomsonfly.com
Doncaster flights to Geneva

Trains

Eurostar
T +44 (0)870 518 6186
W eurostar.com

Rail Europe
T +44 (0)8708 371 371
W raileurope.co.uk

SNCF
T +33 (0)8 92 35 35 35
W voyages-sncf.com

Planning your trip

Buses

Altibus
(Chambéry, Geneva and Lyon)
T +44 (0)820 32 03 68
W altibus.com

Satobus
(Lyon St Exupéry)
T +33 (0)4 27 00 70 07
W satobus-alps.com

Car hire
For parking and garages **>** 146.

Auto Europe
T +44 (0)800 358 1229
W auto-europe.co.uk

Avis
T +44 (0)844 581 0147
W avis.co.uk

Budget
T +44 (0)844 581 9998
W budget.co.uk

easyCar
T +44 (0)8710 500 444
W easycar.co.uk

Europcar
T +44 (0)870 607 5000
W europcar.co.uk

Hertz
T +44 (0)870 850 2677
W hertz.co.uk

holiday autos
T +44 (0)870 400 4461
W holidayautos.co.uk

Private transfers

ATS Airport Transfer Services
T +33 (0)4 50 53 63
W a-t-s.net

The Cool Bus
T +33 (0)6 32 19 29 62
W thecoolbus.co.uk

Threevalleetransfers

T +44 (0)1782 644420
W 3vt.co.uk

Taxis

Altitud'taxi
T +33 (0)4 79 08 15 15

Arolle Taxi
T +33 (0)6 12 28 59 05 or
    +33 (0)4 79 01 09 99

Blanc Le Praz
T +33 (0)4 79 08 41 10

Locatax
T +33 (0)4 79 01 10 10

Prestige des Neiges
T +33 (0)4 79 08 00 81

Station taxis 1850
T +33 (0)4 79 08 23 46

Self-drive

Via michelin route planner
W viamichelin.co.uk

Driving abroad advice
W maddogski.com
W drivingabroad.co.uk

Ferries

Brittany Ferries
From Poole, Portsmouth
and Plymouth
T +44 (0)870 663 2546
W brittany-ferries.com

P&O
From Dover and Portsmouth
T +44 (0)870 598 03 33
W poferries.com

Seafrance
From Dover to Calais
T +44 (0)870 571 17 11
W seafrance.com

Alternatively **ferrybooker.com** and
cheap4ferries.com offer a selection
of fares from various companies.

Insurance

Insure and go
T +44 (0)870 901 3674
W insureandgo.com

Ski Club of Great Britain
T +44 (0)845 601 9422
W skiclubinsurance.co.uk

Ski Insurance
T +44 (0)870 755 6101
W ski-insurance.co.uk

You can also buy insurance
with your lift pass ('carré neige'
– €2.50 per day) which covers you
for recovery from the mountain
without having to prove you're
insured or paying up front (should
you be unfortunate enough to
need it).

Lift passes

If you're very organised, you can
buy your lift passes online (> 26).

Families

Travelling with children? We
recommend booking childcare
(> 139) before you arrive.

Tourist office

T +33 (0)4 79 08 00 29
W courchevel.com
For more information > 154.

This chapter aims to get you **on the piste** as quickly as possible. After all, it's why you're here.

What you'll find in this chapter

Welcome to one of the biggest ski areas in the world. While Paradiski (Les Arcs and La Plagne linked by the Vanoise Express) claims to be the largest, purists insist that the Three Valleys retains the crown, not least for the ease of skiing between the different areas.

In fact, the domain actually has four valleys: Courchevel, Méribel, Val Thorens and Orelle (only relatively recently connected to the lift system).

Skiing here is all about travelling. Competent skiers can set out in the morning and have skied all four valleys by the close of the day. On the other hand, early intermediates can quite happily find more than enough variety without leaving the Courchevel valley all week. If you haven't skied here before, nothing prepares you for the vastness that awaits.

Courchevel's north facing slopes may not be quite as sunny as its neighbour Méribel, but this does mean that the snow tends to stay longer.

Courchevel

1850 is the destination for most people in their first few days. Three long green pistes run into La Croisette (the main lift area). From here, the Verdons gondola takes you to 1850 mid-station where one more lift takes you to Saulire and the Vizelle ridge. From here you can ski to Méribel or take one of a number of reds or blacks back into 1850. (Don't miss **Creux** running between 1650 and 1850 ridges – one of the most enjoyable runs in Courchevel). Mainly beginners and those accessing the accommodation along its four stops use the Jardin Alpin gondola, and Chenus takes you to the top of the ridge above La Tania.

1650 is the furthest point of the Three Valleys and many never make it over here at all. They miss out on some great pistes which often keep their snow longer because there is less traffic.

1550, directly below 1850, has some interesting and challenging runs back to resort and has two lifts connecting it to 1850 (one directly into La Croisette).

La Tania (1350m) gets less sun than the other villages so the pistes can get icy, especially early in the morning, but don't let that put you off. Just two lifts away from Méribel, it's a great base for exploring. Tree lined **Folyères** is one of the loveliest runs in the Alps, although, it can feel more red than blue in icy conditions. **Bouc Blanc/Moretta blanche** is an exhilarating experience, giving you an exceptional long run into the village.

Le Praz, at 1300m, has two of the best blacks in the Three Valleys; **Jean Blanc** and **Jockeys** as well as a long and challenging red (beginners are best taking the bus or the gondola back into the resort). There are two gondolas: Forêt takes you towards to Méribel and Praz to 1850.

Méribel

An absolute joy to ski in good snow, but its south-facing slopes can get slushy in warmer weather and then freeze overnight making them icy first thing: the side of the valley nearest Courchevel gets afternoon sun, so head to the other side in the morning, giving the hard snow time to soften.

Les Menuires and St Martin

Les Menuires – possibly the ugliest resort in the Alps – and St Martin, one of the prettiest, both have long, cruisy, confidence-boosting reds and blues. Particular favourites are **Pramint**, **Jérusalem** and **Allemandes**; for blues don't miss **Pelozet**, **Gros Tougne** and **Petit Creux**.

Val Thorens

At 2300m this is the highest point of the Three Valleys, so don't expect charming tree-lined runs. However, its altitude also helps it retain snow long after the other valleys have lost theirs so it's not

alpineanswers.co.uk

we make booking a ski holiday a pleasureable experience

The ultimate skiers and boarders website brings you up to date information on ski holidays, chalets, hotels, resorts, flexible breaks, late deals, snow reports and much more

D4050

For more information visit our website: **www.alpineanswers.co.uk**
or simply call us on: **020 7801 1080**

all bad. Val Thorens also gives you access to the Orelle valley – a must for good intermediates.

Boarders

Boarders – from total novice to advanced – will find plenty to keep them occupied. Whilst you'll still find some drag lifts, there's usually an alternative: our recommended day trips give details of these.

If you don't like to walk, stay clear of these flatter slopes:

Courchevel
- Middle section of **Bellecôte**
- Last section of **Col de la Loze**
- Last section of **Indiens**

Méribel
- **Boulevard de le Loze**
- The last section of **Truite**

- There are two flattish sections on **Lac de la Chambre**
- **Ours**
- **Sizerin** – too flat even for skiers
- **Villages**

Val Thorens
- The feeder path from **Béranger**
- **Névés**

Les Menuires
- The first section of **Gros Tougne**
- Sections of **Biolley**

Snowparks

The Courchevel snowpark has various different rail and box sections. Two parkers are available to welcome you and give any advice that may be necesary. You will find easy boxes which even kids can try, a line of shaped bumps for both young and old alike and a line of rails for experienced riders.

You can find the snowpark at 1850 at the bottom of the Plantrey chairflift.

Off-piste, back country and heli-skiing

Unless you are an experienced skier and know the area well, you should only ski off-piste with an instructor or mountain guide. All ski schools offer off-piste instruction and guiding, conditions allowing.

'Les Trois Vallées hors piste/off-piste' by Phillippe Baud and Benoît Loucel is a good source for off-piste. (Published by Guide Vamos and available in newsagents in resort).

Heli-skiing is banned in France but you can arrange to fly into nearby Italy or Switzerland with the Bureau des Guides.

ESF also offer off-piste guiding, ski touring and heli-skiing through the Ecole de Hors Piste de l'ESF (> 32).

Ski Prestige

E contact@skiprestige.com
W skiprestige.com
Based in 1850. Group lessons for a maximum group size of five (€150 per person, per day).

Bureau des Guides

T +33 (0)4 79 01 33 66
Heli-skiing prices are around €1200 for four people, two drops and one guide.

Beginners

ZEN areas (Zones d'Evolution des Novices).

These are wide and well protected pistes designed for beginners and families.

1850

ZEN du Practice. Rolling carpet lift (specifically for beginners).
ZEN de Pralong.

1650

ZEN du Mickey.

Le Praz

ZEN de l'Envolée.

Méribel/Mottaret

ZEN du Rossignol.

In La Tania, the Troika draglift is free.

These runs are great for beginners to practise their new found skiing skills:

1850
- **Jardin Alpin (from G3)**, **Bellecôte** and **Verdons** (in that order)
- **Altiport**
- **Biollay** – and cut through to **Jardin Alpin** and **Bellecôte** part way down
- The second half of **Prolong**

1650
- **Grand bosses**
- **Ariondaz** (avoiding the two steep sections to the left of the Bel Air restaurant)
- **Petit bosses** and **Granges** (more like easy blues)
- **Belvedere** is a great beginner run, **Mickeys** is slightly harder

La Tania
- **Col de la Loze**
- **Crêtes**

Lift passes

Each village has a lift pass office (> 27). Photos are no longer required (except for season passes) but age-related discounts (under 14s and over 60s) will need proof of age.

As well as Courchevel-only or a full Three Valleys pass, the lift company has options designed for families and beginners (> 27, **courchevel.com** or the lift offices in resort). A Three Valley pass is best if you plan to leave the valley more than twice (remembering that high winds might shut the linking lifts). Beginners are usually fine with a Courchevel-only pass (you can always buy daily upgrades). Absolute beginners may not need a pass for the first day – check with your ski school.

Online lift passes

Buy your pass online at least 10 days before your first day on the slopes and collect it when you arrive or have it delivered to your hotel or chalet. Go to the 'skiing/snowboarding' section of **courchevel.com**. Passes can be kept from year to year and recharged.

Olympic lift passes

Six day plus passes include a day pass for Val d'Isère/Tignes, Les Arcs/La Plagne, Pralognan-La-Vanoise and Les Saisies (during

the period your pass is valid for).
You need to collect your pass at
the central lift office in the relevant
resort.

Lift pass offices
1850
*La Croisette, 8.45am–4.45pm,
+33 (0)4 79 08 04 09 (7pm on
Saturdays, except at the beginning
and end of the season).
Pralong, Route de l'altiport
8.45am–4.45pm.*

1650
*Maison du Moriond, 8.45am–
4.45pm, +33 (0)4 79 08 08 15
(7pm on Saturdays during peak
periods).
Trois Vallées TS, 8.45am–2.15pm
(4.45pm at weekends).*

1550
*In the Grangettes lift building,
8.45am–4.45pm,
+33 (0)4 79 08 04 09 (7pm on
Saturdays, except at the beginning
and end of the season).*

Le Praz
*Underneath Forêt and Praz
gondolas, 8.35am-5.15pm,
+33 (0)4 79 08 04 09 (7pm on
Saturdays during peak periods).*

La Tania
*Next to the gondola, 8.45am-
4.45pm, +33 (0)4 79 08 04 09.*

Lift closing times
Lift closing times are listed on the
piste map and change in early
February. Bad weather can also
cause early lift closures.

Lost passes
If your pass is handed in, you can
collect it from the Bureau Acceuil
Caisses Remonteés Mechaniques
in La Croisette in 1850 (open
8.35am-5.10pm). If it's not handed
in you will need to buy another one
and claim on your insurance.

Cross-country
There is an extensive
network of cross-country
skiing routes throughout
Courchevel and Méribel. You
can get full details and maps
from the tourist office.

On the Piste

Adult lift pass prices (in €) for the 2007/8 season

No. of days	Courchevel*	Three Valleys	Pedestrian**
1	35	41	14
2	68	81.5	20
3	99	120	26
4	125	153	31
5	148	183	36
6	166	228	46
7	185	228	46
Half day	26.5	33	

* Courchevel to Three Valleys upgrade is €20 a day.

** Pedestrian passes cover all lifts and bus services in Courchevel and Méribel (except the Pass'montagne services). You can also buy one trip passes for €6 – trips down are free!

Avalanche!

Whilst Courchevel has a number of automated explosive systems to prevent avalanches, the danger cannot be completely averted and every year people die on the mountain.

Speed is of the essence if you are caught in an avalanche; if the victim is alive after the initial impact there is an 80% chance of survival if rescued in the first 12 minutes, after 15 minutes the probability of a successful rescue drops dramatically. Your best chance of survival is to be rescued by someone in your own group; a transceiver, shovel and probe are essential kit for off-piste skiing.

Although manufacturers claim that mobile phones cause only minimum interference with transceiver signals, it is also recommended that you switch your mobile off whilst off-piste.

The daily avalanche risk is shown clearly with flags and ratings on a scale of 1-5 throughout the Three Valleys. If in doubt, ask a piste security employee (dressed in black and yellow).

Avalanche risk report
T +33 (0)8 92 68 10 20 (€0.34 per minute)
W avalanches.org

Avalanche warning flags

Yellow Level 1-2
Limited risk

Black/yellow Level 3-4
chequered flag
High risk

5

Black flag Level 5
Very high risk

Rules of the piste

Safety

Most accidents are caused by collisions; it is relatively easy for adults to achieve speeds of over 50kph, even children can quite easily reach 45kph. Above all, be aware of others around you and follow the piste rules.

1. Respect – do not endanger or prejudice the safety of others

2. Control – ski in control, adapting your speed and manner to ability, conditions and traffic. Give way to slower skiers

3. Choice of route – the skier who is further up the slope must choose his route so he does not endanger the skiers below

4. Overtaking – allowed left or right, above or below but always leave sufficient space for the overtaking skier

5. Entering and starting a run – look both up and down the piste before you head off

6. Stopping on the piste – avoid stopping at narrow or low visibility areas. Always stop at the edge of the piste rather than in the middle and make sure that you can be easily seen by approaching skiers

7. Climbing – if you have to walk up or down the piste, do so at the edge and ensure neither you nor your equipment are a danger to anyone else

8. Signs and markings – respect the information given about pistes and the weather

9. Accidents – if you witness an accident, you must give assistance, particularly by alerting piste security

10. Identification – if you are involved in or witness an accident, you must provide your identity to piste security if requested

The International Ski Federation (FIS) Code of Conduct

Emergency telephone numbers

See the inside front cover or a piste map for emergency numbers. In you are involved in an accident, call piste security and give your location as precisely as you can.

If on a piste, it is a good idea to stand your skis or board in the snow above the victim to warn people coming down the hill, particularly if you are below a ridge or around a corner.

Weather

maddogski.com has weather forecasts and reports so you can keep an eye on the snowfall before you arrive in resort. Local radio stations give daily reports; **Radio Nostalgie Courchevel**, 93.2fm and **Radio R' Méribel**, 97.9 and 98.9fm.

Weather can change rapidly in the mountains with bright sunshine deteriorating into cold, low-visibility conditions. Make a habit of checking the weather reports posted in the tourist offices (➤ 154) and at the main lifts (information boards show which runs are open, wind speed and avalanche risk). The top of the right-hand piste markers are painted fluorescent orange to help you in poor visibility.

Ski and snowboard schools

Whilst the largest ski school is the ESF, the number of smaller international ski schools is growing. It is notoriously difficult to become an instructor under the French system, so you can be pretty confident of being taught by an excellent skier whichever school you choose. The main difference with the smaller British schools is (usually) a better command of English, and smaller class sizes. Many people think there is no substitute for being taught by a native speaker of your own language.

If you are holidaying at a peak period (school holidays, Christmas and New Year), book your lessons as early as possible - especially for the British ski schools.

The prices we give here should be used as a guide only – check out individual websites for up-to-date prices.

ESF

The main office is located in La Croisette, 1850.

1850: La Croisette
T +33 (0)4 79 08 07 72
W esfcourchevel.com,
Private tuition: 90 minutes from €70, day from €270 (1-5 people)
Group lessons: from €111 for 4 sessions.
Max. group size: 10 - 12

1650: Maison du Moriond
T +33 (0)4 79 08 26 08
W esfcourchevel1650.com

1550: Rue des Rois
T +33 (0)4 79 08 21 07
W esf-courchevel.com

La Tania
T +33 (0)4 79 08 80 39
W esf-latania.com

Le Praz
T +33 (0)4 79 08 07 72
W esfcourchevel.com
In peak season there are 700 instructors who wear the familiar red ESF uniform in Courchevel – the largest team in France. Whilst you cannot guarantee fluency in English, the sheer number of instructors makes them very flexible in terms of lesson options and availability.

New Generation
Courchevel 1650 and 1850
Immeuble Le Ceylan, 1650, a couple of doors up from Rocky's Bar by the main bus stop.
T +33 (0)4 79 01 03 18,
+44 (0)844 484 3663
W skinewgen.com

Instructors: 37
Private tuition: two hours from €159 (1-2 people), full day from €439 (1-3 people)
Group lessons: from €179 for 4-8 people.
Max. group size: eight
Children: four years and older
A British ski school with predominantly native English speakers and a focus on coaching vs. instruction, New Gen classes revolve around helping you to understand what you need to do so that you can continue improving on your own after ski school has finished. They also have shorter session of 'ski clinics' for those who want to improve their technique.

Supreme

Rue des Verdons, 1850.

T +33 (0)4 79 08 27 87,
  +44 (0)1479 810800

W supremeski.com

Number of instructors: 12

Private tuition: 2 hours from
£110, full day from £290.

Group lessons: from £180
for 4-8 people

Max. group size: nine (10 for
children's classes).

Children: wide range of classes,
including race camps for budding
Olympic champions.

Supreme have been in
Courchevel for 16 years,
making them one of the longest
established British ski schools in
the French Alps. Their instructors
are mostly Brits and the focus is
on less standing around and
more doing!

Magic Snowsports Academy

W magic-courchevel.com
Originally two separate ski
schools (Magic in Motion and
Ski Academy), they have now
combined to form one French-
run ski school with French and
Brit instructors. They have a
particularly good reputation
with children.

Independent instructors

Rob Sewell

Rob has been teaching in
Méribel and Courchevel for the
past 20 years.

T +33 (0)4 79 08 04 17 or
  +33 (0)6 10 14 47 62

Equipment hire

Most hire shops offer similar
equipment at similar prices so
it's best to use somewhere close
to your accommodation or use a
company like Skis Direct or Ski
Higher, that will deliver equipment
to you. If you know what you want
to hire, why not pre-book either
online or with the mobile hire
companies too.

Most shops offer their own
equipment insurance. It's usually
inexpensive and saves you the
hassle of paying up front should
something happen to your skis
or board.

Skis Direct

T +33 (0)6 09 41 21 26
Delivering throughout Courchevel,
Scot Jim Bell will deliver direct

to your accommodation. Phone from the UK or when you arrive in resort.

Ski Higher

Rue des Verdons, 1850 (branches also in Le Praz and La Tania).
T +33 (0)4 79 00 51 70
W skihigher.com
This British-run chain of hire shops has a good range of equipment and offers a helpful and efficient mobile service throughout Courchevel.

Intersport

Les Cascades, 1650.
T +33 (0)4 79 08 31 85
E contact@intersport-courchevel1650.com
W intersport-courchevel1650.com

Skis Location

Résidence Adret, 1550.

T +33 (0)4 79 08 29 96
W skiloc-courchevel.com

Online hire companies

W skiset.com
W sport2000.fr
W twinner.org

Ski kit

Good kit is essential to keep you safe on the slopes. If you have any worries about your equipment, go back to the shop to ask for advice or exchange what you have.

Ski boots

Ski boots can be awkward but they shouldn't be painful. When you try them, wear the socks you're going to ski in and keep your thermals and ski trousers out of the boot. Your feet should feel snug but make sure your toes don't touch the front of the boot when you are in the right skiing position – you should be able to wiggle them easily.

Short toenails are essential - otherwise they bang against the front of the boot.

Snowboard boots

Snowboard boots are easier to walk in and softer than ski boots (and straightforward to fit). They should be tight but not blood stopping; your toes should just touch the end and your heels shouldn't lift too much. The harder, stiffer versions are best for off-piste.

Skis

Most skis these days are carving skis and have a 'waist' so that if you put them on their side and track them in the snow they draw a curve. This helps you turn more easily (rotate or tilt your feet to create an edge) making it quicker to learn and improve.

These skis are generally shorter than non-carving skis though off-piste versions are longer and wider (to help you 'float' in the powder).

The binding of your skis has something called the 'DIN' setting. This dictates how easily the binding releases your boots, helping to avoid knee injuries. Children, beginners and lighter adults will have a lower setting.

Snowboards

Snowboards come in all shapes and sizes to cater for everything from the park (more flexible boards) to off-piste (stiffer) to ski touring (splitboards). If you're a beginner, the rental shop will generally give you a standard shaped board with a normal bindings setup until you know what sort of riding you prefer.

Buy or rent?

The quality of rental equipment is usually pretty good and gives you the chance to try the latest skis. However, if you ski for more than a week or two a year, it's definitely worth investing in custom-fit boots.

If you're thinking of buying your own kit, then end of season sales can see discounts of up to 50%.

Clothing

To adapt as the weather changes, wear layers, carry a hat and an extra fleece in your rucksack, even on sunny days in case the weather closes in. Glasses or goggles with good quality lenses are essential (even on cloudy days) as the sun's rays are reflected by snow and can damage unprotected eyes.

Good gloves or mittens are very important too. Beginners particularly have to consider how waterproof their gloves and trousers are as they can spend a lot of time sitting down with their hands and bum in the snow! If you feel the cold, you can buy thermal glove liners.

Quick routes between resort centres

Don't forget that the bus may be your quickest route, particularly between 1850 and 1650.

Starting point 1850

1650	1550	La Tania (1350)	Le Praz (1300)
Verdons > Verdons > **Biollay** > Pralong or **Mur** > Bd Praméreul > **Praméreul** > Grandes bosses > Indiens	Tovets	Take the path under the bridge to the left of Verdons and Chenus > **Plantrey** > **Crêtes** > Bouc blanc or Bd Arolles > Folyéres or **Moretta blanche**	Take the path under the bridge to the left of Verdons and Chenus > **Brigues** > **Bd Amoureux**

Starting point 1650

1850	1550	La Tania (1350)	Le Praz (1300)
Ariondaz >	**Ariondaz** >	**Ariondaz** >	**Ariondaz** >
Ariondaz >	Ariondaz >	Ariondaz >	Ariondaz >
Petite Bosse >	**Petite Bosse** >	**Petite Bosse** >	**Petite Bosse** >
Bd Gravelles >	Bd Gravelles >	Bd Gravelles >	Bd Gravelles >
Gravelles >	**Gravelles** >	**Gravelles** >	**Gravelles** >
Altiport >	Altiport >	Altiport But keep	Altiport >
Bellecôte	Bellecôte >	high and cut through	Bellecôte >
	Tovets	towards **Verdons** >	Take the path under
		Coqs >	the bridge to the left of
		Lanches >	Verdons and Chenus >
		Or **Crêtes Folyéres** or	**Brigues** >
		Moretta blanche	**Bd Amoureux**

Starting point 1550

1850	1650	La Tania (1350)	Le Praz (1300)
Tovets or Grangettes	Tovets or Grangettes > Verdons > Verdons > **Biollay** > Pralong or **Mur** > Bd Praméreul > **Praméreul** > Grandes bosses > Indiens	Tovets or Grangettes > Turn right off the lift and ski over the small bridge > Plantrey > Crêtes > **Bouc blanc** or Bd Arolles > Folyéres or **Moretta blanche**	Tovets or Grangettes > Turn right off the lift and ski over the small bridge > **Brigues** > **Bd Amoureux**

Starting point La Tania (1350)

1850	1650	1550	Le Praz (1300)
La Tania > Dou des Lanches > **Col de la Loze** > **Lac Bleu** > Loze Est	La Tania > Dou des Lanches > **Col de la Loze** > **Lac Bleu** > Verdons > Halfway down Verdons: > **Biollay** > Pralong or **Mur** > Bd Praméreul > **Praméreul** > Grandes bosses > Indiens	La Tania > **Col de la Loze** > **Lac Bleu** > Verdons > Tovets	La Tania > Bottom half of **Bouc Blanc** > **Murettes**

Starting point Le Praz (1300)

1850	1650	1550	La Tania (1350)
Praz > Turn left immediately out of the gondola > Epicea > Cut across **Dou du midi** to the path opposite which leads to 1850 centre	Forêt > Crêtes > **Lac Bleu** > Verdons > Halfway down Verdons: > **Biollay** > Pralong or **Mur** > Bd Praméreul > **Praméreul** > Grandes bosses > Indiens	Praz > Cut across **Dou du midi** to the path opposite which leads to 1850 centre. Ski under the bridge to the left of La Croisette > **Tovets**	Forêt > **Bd Arolles** > **Folyéres** or **Moretta blanche**

Piste rankings

Pistes can sometimes be confusing – a red run can feel more 'black' than 'red' and vice versa, and for more experienced skiers looking for moguls or steeps, the piste ranking system is too broad to really be useful.

Mad Dog teamed up with New Generation (> 32) ski school to rank the red and black pistes in the Three Valleys using a star system (* = easier and *** = more challenging).

Apart from gradient and width, there are other factors to consider:

- North or south: north-facing slopes are more inclined to be icy, but keep snow longer

- Traffic – less busy pistes can keep their snow longer but may not be pisted as often

- Grooming – the easier blues and greens tend to be pisted more frequently than the reds and blacks – some pistes are never groomed at all

- Weather – has there been recent snow? Is it windy?

The piste rankings

- Pistes are listed in alphabetical order by valley, reds first, then blacks

- Connecting lifts are in CAPITALS

Red pistes – Courchevel

Piste	Comments
Bd Amoureux **	Runs into Le Praz. Regularly snow cannoned to keep it open. Fairly flat but can be icy. Continuation of **Brigues** and **Jean Blanc.**
Bel Air *	Always well groomed, a wide longish red with fairly even pitch all the way down. BEL AIR
Bouc Blanc **	Two entrances – the steeper one is higher up the piste. The second entrance avoids the very top pitch, which is quite exposed and can get icy and rocky. In good snow, this is a joy to ski – wide and open all the way down towards La Tania. LOZE, PLANTREY, BOUC BLANC
Brigues **/***	The gradient, camber and direction change all the way down. North-facing, it can get icy in windy, cold weather. Snow cannons keep it is open pretty much all season. Runs from the bottom of EPICEA and PLANTREY
Cave des Creux **	South-facing, the bottom pitch can get bare in warm weather. Often quiet. GRAVELLES
Chapelets **	Steep top pitch which can get icy and quite mogulled. Not always groomed. In good conditions, this is one of the most fun reds in Courchevel, with varying pitches all the way down. SIGNAL

Piste	Comments
Combe Pylônes ***	Steep all the way down, but you can avoid the top pitch by taking a path which re-joins the piste part way down, and also gives an escape route halfway down onto **Combe Saulire**. (Ski past the top of the piste to access the path). If you fall in icy conditions, be prepared to slide! VIZELLE, SUISSES, MARMOTTES, CREUX NOIRS
Combe Saulire **/***	Three entrances – the easiest is the path to the right of the central entrance as you stand at the top. The most challenging steep and narrower entrance is on the far left (only accessible from SAULIRE). Busy at the end of the day as people come back into the resort. VIZELLE, SUISSES, SAULIRE, MARMOTTES, CREUX NOIRS
Combe Roc Mugnier ***	Avoid the steepest top part by taking a path entrance to the right – although this is also quite steep. In icy conditions you may feel like you are just linking slides unless you have really good edges. ROC MUGNIER
Creux *	Probably the easiest red in Courchevel. Long and wide with something for everyone – wide open spaces at the top, fabulous views, ski through the trees at the bottom. It can get busy. The bottom half is in the shade till late morning early in the season so the snow can change from top to bottom. VIZELLE, SUISSES, SAULIRE, MARMOTTES, CREUX NOIRS
Dou du midi ***	Long run from 1850 to 1550. Steep (but wide) part at the top which earns it *** - otherwise it is a great run where you can feel a sense of achievement at the bottom. LOZE, PLANTREY, BOUC BLANC

Piste	Comments
Dev. 1550 *	Runs off **Brigues** and **Jean Blanc**
Jean Pachod ***	Fantastic in good conditions but it's rare for it to be good all the way down. Quite variable terrain – steep, then a narrow path leads onto a wider section which can get small moguls or rocky. The sun is on this run late morning to afternoon. CHANROSSA, ROC MERLET
Lac Creux *	This is a path connecting two pistes. Runs off **Creux**.
Lanches ***	There's not a lot going for this access route to La Tania. Steep start, followed by a flat path and a wider part with an odd camber, before it joins **Bouc Blanc**. PRAZ JUGET, CRETES, COQS, CHENUS
Marmottes ***	The top pitch is probably more ** but lower down it can get steep and bumpy. It has been widened in recent years to make it easier. VIZELLE, SUISSES, MARMOTTES, CREUX NOIRS
Marquetty ***	Short but bumpy and hardly ever pisted. Can get icy. BIOLLAY
Mur ***	This means 'wall' in French, probably because of the two steep parts, punctuated by flatter sections. Facing south, it can suffer in warm weather. Not always pisted. Runs off **Altiport**.
Murettes **/***	Beautiful run in good conditions – down through the trees to Le Praz. Two access points both similar in difficulty. In icy conditions this warrants a *** rating. Runs off **Jockeys** and **Moretta blanche**.

Piste	Comments
Park City **	Wide and steep. Great views towards 1650. AIGUILLE DE FRUIT
Petit Dou **	Classic red. Often quiet despite coming into the centre of 1850. LOZE, PLANTREY
Petit Lac **	Short run which doesn't get much sun. BIOLLAY, PRALONG
Rama ***	Similar to **Marmottes**. The bottom half can get messy at the end of the day. Runs off **Park City**.
Rochers * & ***	The top half is *, the steeper bottom half ***. Tends to be quiet. SIGNAL
Roches Grises ***	Steep and bumpy – great if that's your thing. CREUX NOIRS
Roc Merlet **	Very short red run. ROC MERLET, CHANROSSA

Black pistes – Courchevel

Piste	Comments
Chanrossa **	Steep for the top two-thirds. Doesn't get too busy. The bottom third flattens out with rollers – keep your speed up. ROC MERLET, CHANROSSA
Couloir de Belges ***	Bumpy, narrow and unpisted at the top – watch out for rocks except in good snow. Widens out after the initial entrance. The snow can get hard. VIZELLE, SUISSES, MARMOTTES, CREUX NOIRS
Dou de Lanches **	Originally a red run, there are only two steep pitches on this run – you can avoid the second icier section by cutting through to **Bouc Blanc** on the right after the first steep section. Try not to fall on the lower section as it is right under the Dou de Lanches chair! DOU DE LANCHES
Grand Couloir ***	This infamous black is allegedly the steepest in Europe – nearly 40 degrees in the top section. It's certainly one of the hardest in the Three Valleys. After the nerve-wracking narrow ridge – the only way in – you then have to deal with steep bumps, which can be lethal in icy conditions. It gets more crowded on Fridays as many people wait till the end of the week before they attempt it. SAULIRE
Jean Blanc **	Together with Jockeys, this is what blacks are all about; varied terrain, steep sections, tree-lined (so usually excellent for low visibility conditions). Part way down, you can get onto Brigues to Le Praz or Deviation to reach 1550. PLANTREY, BOUC BLANC, LOZE

Piste	Comments
Jockeys **	Jockeys leads off **Bouc Blanc** just above the La Tania gondola. see **Jean Blanc**. PLANTREY, LOZE, BOUC BLANC
M **	The last pitch can get icy. VIZELLE, SUISSES, MARMOTTES, CREUX NOIRS
Suisses *	Lots of different entrance options – if you come in under the chair, you will be taking *** route with a more gentle entrance from **Marmottes** or the top of AIGUILLE DE FRUIT. VIZELLE, SUISSES, MARMOTTES, CREUX NOIRS
Turcs *	Short run linking pistes. VIZELLE, SUISSES, MARMOTTES, CREUX NOIRS

Red pistes – Méribel

Piste	Comments
Alouette **	Narrow and steep at the top. The top gets lots of sun which affects the snow in warmer weather. PLATTIÈRES 3, ALLAMANDS, GRANGES
Blaireau *	Lovely, always well-groomed and easier than some blues (including **Faon** alongside it). TOUGNÈTE, ST MARTIN 1 & 2
Bd. Challe **	Cut-through path. ROC DE TOUGNE 1 & 2, TEPPES
Bouvreuil **	First section – after the bottom of Côte Brune lift – can get slushy when it's warm. PLATTIÈRES 2
Buse **/***	Cut-through path but steep and narrow. CHERFERIE
Campagnol **	Easiest of the two Mont Vallon reds but steep drop off from the narrow path at the top. MONT VALLON
Cerf ***	Great run but steep; if you fall you may slide all the way down! BURGIN 1
Chamois *	Long wide run. You can easily cut through to **Biche** at most points, though there is little difference between them. SAULIRE, VIZELLE, SUISSES, MARMOTTES, BURGIN 2, GRAND ROSIERE, COMBE
Combe Vallon ***	Fantastic long run down from Mont Vallon, always mogulled – often quite challenging. MONT VALLON
Coqs **	Cut-through between runs. Always pisted. COMBES

Piste	Comments
Dahu ***	*** because access is via the steepest part of **Combe Tougnète** (albeit this is one of the easiest blacks in the Three Valleys). One of the first runs to lose snow later in the season. Access via **Combe Tougnète**.
Ecureuil ***	Steeper than **Combe Tougnète** which offers a similar route – not always pisted. TOUGNÈTE
Fouine **	Lovely red, quite steep but always pisted – usually has great snow. Access from **Martre**.
Lac de la Chambre **	Long and varied. Can get busy. Two sections where you need to schuss but you can see them coming. CÔTE BRUNE, 3 VALLÉES, BOUQUETIN
Lagopède ***	Steep red – great pitch all the way down. ROC DE TOUGNE 1 & 2, TEPPES
Marcassin **	Steep but sustained pitch all the way down. SAULIRE, VIZELLE, SUISSES, MARMOTTES, BURGIN 2, GRAND ROSIERE, COMBE
Mauduit ***	Named after local skier, Georges Mauduit. It was re-classified from black after some chalets were built at the top of the village. Can be icy at the bottom where you reach the trees. Not always pisted. SAULIRE, VIZELLE, SUISSES, MARMOTTES, BURGIN 2, GRAND ROSIERE, COMBE
Mouflon **	Nice classic red. PLATTIÈRES 3, ALLAMANDS, GRANGES
Niverolle **/***	Warrants *** if icy. Starts gently but the bottom section is very steep. SAULIRE, VIZELLE, SUISSES, MARMOTTES, BURGIN 2, GRAND ROSIERE, COMBE

Piste	Comments
Renard ***/**	Top half (from Dent de Burgin) is ***; after it crosses **Bd de la Loze** it is usually ** but is not always pisted. Check it out from the chairlift and take **Geai** if you don't like the look of it. DENT DE BURGIN
Venturon **	Fantastic run down in the Méribel – Mottaret valley. Can be a little steep at the top. CÔTE BRUNE, 3 VALLÉES, BOUQUETIN

Black pistes – Méribel

Piste	Comments
Bartavelle **	Excellent bumps off to one side. Warrants *** if not pisted. Access from Lagopède
Bosses ***	Long run with brilliant moguls pretty much all the way down. It gets the sun in the morning. Never pisted so only go down if you are a serious bumps fan. It's quite a public place to fall as it runs alongside Plan de l'homme. PLAN DE L'HOMME, ARPASSON
Chevreuil **	Can get bumpy and icy but great when pisted. There is a section which goes off camber at the bottom; watch out for those pylons! Runs off **Lièvre**.
Combe Tougnète **/*	Steep but wide entrance which can get icy. After that it flattens out into a red-level piste. TOUGNÈTE
Face **	Usually pisted but narrow. Always soft in the morning as it gets early sun. OLYMPIC
Grand Rosière ***	Can get mega-icy – beware! It can also have great bumps. Access is halfway down **Niverolle**.
Sanglier **	Lovely run, wide and fun all the way down. If it is pisted it moves down to *. SAULIRE, VIZELLE, SUISSES, MARMOTTES, BURGIN 2, GRAND ROSIERE, COMBE
Tetras **	Varied, interesting run, including a wide bumps section. Snow can get worn in warm weather. Usually quiet. LOZE, DOU DE LANCHE, COL DE LA LOZE

Red pistes – Les Menuires and St Martin

Piste	Comments
4 Vents *	Lovely run, though there's a steep section towards the bottom. Access from **Bd de la lance** and **Mont de la Chambre**.
Allamands *	Cruisy red all the way to Les Menuires. One or two steep parts but they are always on wide sections. ALLAMANDS, PLATTIÈRES 3
Becca **	Nice run. BECCA
Bd de la lance *	Link piste.
Combes ***	Can be icy and also is one of the first slopes to get worn in less perfect conditions. Access from **Liason** and **David Douillet Haut**.
Crêtes **	MASSE 2
David *** Douillet Haut & Bas	Gets icy, bumpy and busy. As a consequence, can be one of the first to get worn if it hasn't snowed for a while. The piste is named after a gold medal judo champion who skis here with his family. MONT DE LA CHAMBRE, BRUYERES 2, CÔTE BRUNE
Fred Covili **	Fred Covili is a Grand Slalom world champion who hails from Les Menuires. This run is a classic red; usually it has great snow. MASSE 2

Piste	Comments
Jérusalem *	Long cruisy red which is often cited as a favourite. It can be stony after the narrow section between two rocks part way down. The bottom is not cannoned so snow texture can be quite different. Keep your speed up at the bottom. ST MARTIN 2, CHERFERIE, TOUGNÈTE
Les enverses **/***	Nice long run which is a little steeper towards the bottom. Runs from bottom of MASSE.
Liason **	Cut-through path between pistes, but can be narrow and icy in places. Access from Lac des Combes from the top of BECCA.
Montaulever **	The last pitch gets very busy which can create moguls. It also gets the sun so will have softer snow in warmer weather. BRUYERES 1
Pramint **	Another classic red run with a few fun rollers towards the bottom. You can cut out part way down into Pelozet which rejoins at the bottom of the piste. ST MARTIN 2, TOUGNÈTE
Rochers *	MASSE
Teppes *	TEPPES, ROC DE TOUGNE 1 & 2

Black pistes – Les Menuires and St Martin

Piste	Comments
3 Marches **	Not often skied as you just end up back at the same chair. Icy first thing. ALLAMANDS, PLATTIÈRES 3
Aiglon **	Quite short, but often stony and exposed to the wind. ETÉLÉ
Dame blanche ***	One of the hardest blacks in the Three Valleys; mostly icy and very steep and can be bumpy too. MASSE
Etélé ***	Can be very bumpy, never groomed. ETÉLÉ
Lac Noir **	Runs on from **Crêtes** from the top of MASSE 2
Léo Lacroix **/***	Top section is steepest and most challenging. Runs off **Bd de la lance** and **David Douillet Haut**.
Masse **	Short, steep section at the top. MASSE 2
Pylônes ***	Never groomed, gets mogulled. MONT DE LA CHAMBRE
Rocher Noir **	Nice run. ROCHER NOIR

Red pistes - Val Thorens

Piste	Comments
Béranger ***	There are four red options from the top of the Funitel Peclet; **Béranger** is the most difficult followed by **Lac Blanc**, then Christine then **Tête Ronde**. Each pair tends to be pisted on alternate days. As you go up in the Funitel, check which one has not been pisted. **Béranger** has a cut-through path on the left which is flatter but not always pisted. GLACIER, FUNITEL PECLET
Bd Cumin *	Short steepish bit at the start but then a lovely flattish path run through the valley to Les Menuires. You may want to take it more slowly if you don't like narrow pistes. Not so easy for novice boarders. From the bottom of BOISMINT.
Boismint **	BOISMINT
Bouchet **	Highest point in the four valleys and an access point for the Bouchet Glacier off-piste itinerary. BOUCHET
Chamois ***	Should be black but probably graded red as it's the only route back to the Val Thorens valley from Rosaël. It's not for the faint-hearted and in less perfect conditions it's not unusual to see people crying! There's a narrow path if you want to avoid the steep top pitch. FUNITEL, GRAND FOND, ROSAËL
Christine */**	See **Béranger**. GLACIER, FUNITEL PECLET

Piste	Comments
Col **	Keep your speed up off the chairlift to get to the top of the piste. Extremely dangerous to go off piste here as it's surrounded by a glacier. There may be mogul on the top section. COL
Col de l'audzin ***	Great run with a 900m vertical drop. Because it's long, less experienced skiers may want to take it easy. Check out conditions from the cable car or on the daily piste map. CIME CARON
Falaise **	It can be easy to miss the access from **Chamois**.
Glacier **/***	North-facing slope, usually not busy so often has some of the best snow in the valley. *** rating is due to the steepness. GLACIER
Haute Combe **/***	South-facing piste so the condition depends mainly on the weather. BOISMINT
Lac blanc **	See **Béranger**. Steep section in the middle. FUNITEL PECLET, GLACIER
Mauriennaise **	South-facing, so the condition is variable. Escape route onto a blue towards the bottom of the piste. ROSAËL
Médaille *	Lovely run. FUNITEL GRAND FOND
Névés */**	Cut through between pistes. Access from **Combe de caron**.
Plan de l'eau ***	Long steep section in the middle. PLAN DE L'EAU

Piste	Comments
Portette **/***	Sometimes icy. Under the lift can get bumpy. PORTETTE
Rhodos **/***	Quite often unpisted. Follows on from **Médaille**.
Tête ronde *	See **Béranger**. FUNITEL PECLET, GLACIER
Variante **/***	If it's windy at the top, the first pitch can be icy. FUNITEL GRAND FOND

Black pistes – Val Thorens

Piste	Comments
Arolle **	Great bumps run – not pisted. MOUTIERE
Cascades ***	Great bumps run – not pisted. CASCADES
Combe de caron **/***	Absolute must – a great black with fabulous views and a long run down the mountain. Can be bumps in places and a few steeper sections. CIME CARON
Combe Rosaël **/***	Its south-facing position makes the snow more variable. The bumps which build up on this run can get slushy in warm weather. CIME CARON
Marielle Goitschel */**	Two entrances – the right-hand one (go along the flat section at the top) is easier. Can get bumpy on the left. 3 VALLÉES, CÔTE BRUNE

Day trips

There are lots of great routes helping you explore the Three Valleys; here are just two of our favourites and you can download more on **maddogski.com**, including:

- The Méribel villages
- Méribel, Mottaret and Mont Vallon
- Les Menuires and La Masse
- The fourth valley

The Three Valleys escapade

This challenge, designed by the tourist office as a great way to discover the Three Valleys, reaches the furthest points of the ski domain including the top of the glaciers in Orelle and Val Thorens. Pick up a plan and route map from the lift office or tourist office.

For good skiers who know the area, with a little planning the escapade can be done in one day, or you can cover it at a more leisurely pace over a few days. Follow the symbols on the piste map (yellow arrows on a small green circle) collecting a stamp at each of the 14 checkpoints; they're all different so you can't cheat! If you're planning to do this in one day, make sure you take sandwiches to eat on the go. On completion, you can proudly collect your certificate at the lift office and also buy an 'exclusive' medal for €7.

About the day trips

Aim to start these trips around 9am, avoiding the ski school queues that start to build up from 9.30am at the main lifts (schools have priority queuing). Timings are based on the pace of a competent red-run skier and assume good conditions and average lift queues. Allow additional time if you are skiing more slowly or during school holidays when lifts can have longer waiting times. If you're leaving the Courchevel valley, it's better to be less ambitious than to miss the last connecting lift home, which can result in a very expensive taxi fare.

All piste directions assume you are facing downhill; lift directions refer to the way you are facing as you get off.

Our researchers have worked hard to make these itineraries as accurate as possible. However, pistes and routes can change from season to season so please take a piste map with you in case anything is unclear.

Day trip 1
– The Courchevel Valley

This is a good first day on the slopes starting with a short section of an easy green to get your ski legs back. It takes in all five villages, starting and finishing in 1850 – if you're in Le Praz or La Tania, you will probably find it easiest to join at 1850 mid-station. Lunch is at Bel Air in 1650 (you will need to book). If you want a cheaper option, eat in the village of 1650 or take sandwiches.

Lift	Comments
Verdons	One of the gondolas coming from the centre of 1850. At the top turn left or right to take **Verdons**, watching for signs for Biollay part way down.
Biollay	At the top, turn left or right and take **Biollay** back down to Coqs, next to Biollay.
Coqs	Turn right at the top of this lift onto **Loze Est**. Pass the top of Crêtes (chairlift) on your left, and turn about 150m past the top of the Bouc Blanc to take **Bouc Blanc**. (There is a slightly easier access a short distance down the piste on the left.) Halfway down, you have a choice of taking **Folyères** or the rest of **Bouc Blanc**. **Folyères** (on the left) is incredibly pretty but can get icy so is not always an easier option.
	If you take **Bouc Blanc** you will pass the La Tania Stade (competition piste) on your right. Just pass this, cut through to **Folyères** via a path on the left (just past the bottom of Bouc Blanc drag lift). Keep your speed up as you come into resort, watching out for beginners. Ski under the bridge on the right to La Tania gondola.
La Tania	Turn right at the top and ski under the bridge for Dou des Lanches.
Dou des Lanches	Turn right at the top for a coffee break.
Break	**Le Roc Tania** (> 109).

Lift	Comments
Col de la Loze	Keep your speed up at the end, bearing right of the rock towards **Lac Bleu**, which turns left and joints **Loze Est**. This doubles back on itself (don't go straight ahead to 1850). At the end of the tree-lined path take Sources (drag).
Sources ⛷	Turn left at the top and head to mid-station to take Saulire.
Saulire 🚡	Follow the piste, keeping right at junctions, to the ridge between Courchevel and Méribel. On the ridge keep left and take **Creux** (an outstanding run through the valley between 1850 and 1650). Halfway down, the piste separates; keep right until you reach two chairlifts (one on either side) – take the one on the right.
Chanrossa 🚡	At the top, ski straight ahead into the 1650 domain onto **Roc Merlet**. At the bottom of the piste, just by the bottom of Roc Merlet chairlift, you join **Montagnes Russes**. Just past the 11 marker on this piste, bear right crossing the Pyramides double drag and onto **Pyramides**. Keep bearing right onto **Pyramide Ariondaz**. The first stretch is quite flat so keep your speed up till you reach the junction at the top of Roc Mugnier chairlift. Cross over the junction with Grandes Bosses.

Lift	Comments
Lunch	**Le Bel Air restaurant** (pre-book) +33 (0)4 79 08 00 93 (**>** 108).
	Come out of the restaurant; ski down and right onto **Ariondaz**. When you can see the Signal chair cut across keeping La Casserole restaurant on your left and join **Indiens** to the right of the restaurant. This takes you towards 1650. You can take **Marquis** on your left or keep straight ahead taking **Belvedère** into 1650 heading for the main cable car/gondola station on the left at the bottom of the slopes
Ariondaz	Turn right out of the lift cutting straight across the slopes, taking care at this busy junction. Take **Ariondaz Petits Bosses**, and, as the path comes around, bear right and join the last part of **Grandes Bosses** to Petit Bosses drag to the left of La Casserole. More experienced skiers can drop off the path into the top of a small gully (only in good snow conditions) coming out by La Casserole and Petit Bosses drag
Petit Bosses	This is an easy beginners' drag lift; turn left at the top onto **Bd Gravelles** which leads down to four lifts. There's a very short red section at the end
Gravelles	Head for the right-hand lift on the opposite side. Take **Altiport** down and over two rollers. If you're tired keep your speed up to join **Bellecôte** to 1850 and miss out the next two lifts. You rejoin the itinerary at La Croisette, skiing under the bridge to take **Tovets** or **Dou du Midi** to 1550. Otherwise keep left and take Suisses chairlift

On the Piste

Lift	Comments
Suisses 🚠	Turn hard right immediately at the top. Ski down a ridge until you reach the entrance to **Couloir de Belges** on your left or **Combe Pylônes** lower down on your left. To avoid the steeper upper part of **Pylônes**, continues past the top of the piste and take a path which comes around the peak to your left. This joins the piste part way down. Both the red and the black routes meet at the mid-station.
Vizelle 🚡 OR **Saulire** 🚡	If you want one more run, head back up the mountain to ski **Combe Saulire** which has three entrances – the most difficult entrance is only accessible via Saulire – the other two are best accessed from Vizelle. At mid-station keep skiing down via **Verdons** to reach 1850 and La Croisette. Head left under the bridge. Take **Tovets** straight ahead or keep left and take **Dou du Midi** (keeping Plantrey chairlift on your left) all the way down to 1550.
Break	Take a break at **L'Oeil du Boeuf** opposite the flags at the bottom of the piste (➤ 87).
Tovets 🚠	Takes you back to 1850.
Final stop	**Bar le Jump**, 1850 (➤ 93).

Day trip 2 –
St Martin de Belleville

This itinerary takes you to the charming village of St Martin de Belleville and onto the edge of Les Menuires. The route goes through Méribel and up and over into the third valley, taking in some lovely cruisy blues and reds. On the way home you have the option to ski up to three black pistes, two of which are relatively easy.

Lift	Comments
Verdons	Turn back on yourself as you leave the lift to ski **Verdons** as far as Coqs chairlift.
Coqs	From the top turn left towards the short two-man Col de la Loze chair.
Col de la Loze	Head straight ahead off the lift, then take Bd de la Loze into the Méribel valley. (Boarders may prefer to reach Méribel by going over the Saulire ridge as this is a flattish run). Head right to take Belette at the junction, running down to join Rhodos, Doron and into the Méribel centre.
Tougnète 1 & 2	If you like skiing blacks, check out the condition of the slope under the first section of this lift, as there is an opportunity to ski it on the way home. Turn right from the gondola taking Crêtes along a ridge till you reach Jérusalem on the left-hand side. Follow this fantastic cruisy red all the way down, keep your speed up as it flattens out and you head left to join Verdet. This brings you out near two restaurants and St Martin 2 (chair).

Lift	Comments
Break	**Le Chardon Bleu** (> 111) – just next to the top of St Martin 1 gondola. You'll be returning here to lunch at the opposite restaurant just further up the slopes. After your break, follow the gentler **Biolley** all the way down to St Martin. St Martin 1 is on your left as you reach the village.
St Martin 1	At the top, cross the slope to take St Martin 2.
St Martin 2	Turn right from the top following **Gros Tougne** all the way until you can see the lifts and village of Les Menuires. Take Combes chair ahead of you in the centre of the village.
Combes	Turn left at the top to take **l'Allée** as far as Allamands chair.
Allamands	Follow **Grand Lac**. If you have time before lunch take **Teppes** drag lift and **Teppes** to rejoin **Grand Lac**, until it joins **Pelozet** taking you all the way down le Corbeleys for lunch.
Lunch	**Le Corbeleys** +33 (0)4 79 08 95 31 (> 112) – on your left just above the bottom of St Martin 2 chair.

Lift	Comments
St Martin 2 🚡	At the top you have a choice – **Combe de Tougnète** whose steep entrance is the most difficult part of the piste, or **Ecureuil**. They both join up at the Tougnète mid-station. Follow **Lièvre** into Méribel. If some of your group want to ski another black take **Chevreuil** under Tougnète gondola. Meet up at the Burgin-Saulire gondola.
Burgin-Saulire 🚠	At the top, ski round to the right to take **Creux** down the ridge which runs between 1850 and 1650. At the bottom take Gravelles chair back to 1850, 1550, Le Praz and La Tania (Praméreul if you're heading home to 1650). If you're tired, ski **Combe Saulire** instead, joining **Verdons** into 1850. A good stop on the way home is Le Chalet des Pierres (**>** 106) on your right as you ski the last part of **Verdons**. Whilst it's not cheap to sit on the sunny terrace, they have cheaper drinks in the side bar.
Gravelles 🚡	Turn right and ski **Altiport** with its two rollers and flat section taking you into **Bellecôte** and down into 1850. If you fancy one more black run, head left at the bottom of the rollers to take Suisses chairlift.
Suisses 🚡	**Suisses** has varying levels of difficulty – (**>** 48).
Break	As you enter the last tree and chalet lined section in 1850 of **Bellecôte** stop at **le Courcheneige** (on the left) or **la Bergerie** (on the right **>** 95).

Where to find the best **food and drink** in resort and on the mountain, from regional specialities to luxurious restaurants.

What you'll find in this chapter

Courchevel has some of the best restaurants in the Alps. As well as gourmet Savoyard specialities, you'll find a wide choice from oyster bars to Italian and Asian cuisine.

Special diets

I am vegetarian
Je suis vegetarian(ne)

...but I can eat fish
mais je peux manger des poissons

I cannot eat nuts/dairy products/wheat
Je ne peux pas manger des noix/des produits laitiers/du blé

Despite its reputation, it is possible to eat well in Courchevel without blowing your budget – although bar prices tend to be on par with London, particularly in the more upmarket bars in 1850.

If you would like water with your meal, the local tap water is perfectly safe and also delicious as it comes from the mountain. Ask for a *'carafe d'eau'*.

Finally, don't feel you have to eat in the village in which you are staying. There is a free, efficient bus service until midnight so it's easy to explore.

What's at steak?

Carnivores have a treat in store. Fantastic steaks are available at reasonable prices in many establishments – our favourites are 'L'Oeil de Boeuf in 1550 and Le Darbeilo in Le Praz.

Blue	bleu
Rare	saignant (pronounced 'sanyon')
Medium	à point
Well-done	bien cuit
Steak tartare	raw minced beef mixed with onions, herbs and spices
Pavé	thick cut rump steak
Entrecôte	similar to rib eye – fatty but flavoursome
Faux-filet	similar to sirloin
Filet	similar to fillet steak
Côte de boeuf	a huge side of beef normally served on the bone with sauces and shared between two or more people

Show some respect

Hundreds of glaciers have melted in the last 150 years.

Join our Respect the Mountain campaign to save those still standing.

Buy a green wristband and visit **respectthemountain.com** to discover how you can make a difference.

respectthemountain.com

Savoyard food

Beaufort	a hard cheese made from the milk of the local mahogany-coloured Beaufort cows
Chevrotin	a soft, almost sweet goats cheese that is perfect after a meal with some wine or port
Crozets	tiny squares of pasta that are traditionally served in a sauce of local cheese, ham and cream
Diots	local sausages – usually quite a strong flavour – in plain, cheese or cabbage variations and definitely an acquired taste
Emmental de Savoie	a classic tawny-coloured 'holey' mountain cheese
Fondue	either a bubbling cauldron of oil that you cook chunks of meat in or else a molten mix of cheeses and spirits to dip bread into. Normally ordered for two or more
Raclette	a grill with a large lump of cheese is brought to your table. As the cheese melts, scrape it onto cold meats, potatoes and salad. Normally ordered for two or more
Reblochon	a local cheese that has a delicious flavour and an easily recognisable pungent smell – you'll smell it in all Savoyard restaurants. Originally made with the milk from the second milking (the rebloche)
Pierre chaude	a hot stone on which you cook a variety of meats on your table. Sprinkle the stone with salt before cooking to prevent sticking
Tartiflette	an extremely satisfying mix of potato, bacon, cream and reblochon cheese which is then baked in the oven. A variation: Tartichèvre is made with goat's cheese
Tomme de Savoie	an ivory-coloured, delicate cheese often made with skimmed milk and therefore lower in fat

Vegetarian options

As always in France, if you are vegetarian finding something to eat other than pizza or pasta is a challenge; many restaurants just don't seem to understand the concept of vegetarian food. Of course, Savoyard cuisine excels in cheese and there are some great dishes such as salade de chevre chaud (goats cheese salad) and cheese fondues and raclettes to be sampled – all made out of local cheeses.

We've tried the vegetarian dishes in all of the restaurants reviewed in this section – those that offer more than the standard fare have a **V** but don't expect the wider range you have in the UK.

In terms of accommodation, catered chalet holidays are usually a good option for vegetarians; you'll at least get some variety throughout the week.

Children

Children are welcome in all restaurants and most places will have a special kids' menu or half portions on offer. Our favourite family-friendly restaurants are listed in **Children** > 142.

Budget meals and take-aways

You can usually tell by the appearance of a restaurant whether it will break the bank or not, although even the top end places often have good value fixed price menus. Most of the pizza restaurants and British bars offer cheaper meals.

If you fancy a night in, try Le Passage in 1850 for pizza, salads, crêpes and sandwiches. In 1650 La Ferme des Saveurs (> 92) has a different *'plat du jour'* each day, which you can pre-order. Ready-roasted chickens, raclette and fondue are all on the menu. Further down the mountain in La Tania, Snow food has a pizza and panini style menu.

There are a number of designated picnic areas with tables and chairs throughout Courchevel – or you can just improvise by sitting on upturned skis or boards. For colder days use the indoor

Food and drink

picnic halls at mid-station 1850 and next to the lift pass office in 1650.

If you want to picnic on the piste but don't want to carry it around until lunch time **Picnics on the Piste** (picnicsonthepiste.com) will deliver your picnic to you at a pre-arranged meeting point.

Resort restaurants

The high number of catered chalets in Courchevel can make it difficult to get a table on the staff night off (usually Wednesday or Thursday). Restaurants often have two sittings and it's best to make your reservation soon after you arrive so that you get the time that suits you.

Drink	
Chartreuse	loopy juice in the shape of a spirit – especially nice when added to hot chocolate (green chaud)
Demi	beer is generally drunk in halves in France – sometimes served with peach syrup (demi pêche) – much nicer than it sounds! A larger beer is called un serieux. Ask for a pression if you would like draft lager.
Eau de vie	a *digestif* (so called because it is supposed to aid digestion). Good ones are delicious but bad ones can be akin to petrol!
Génépi	famous for its local digestive values (when taken in moderation!), this local tipple is made from the Génépi flower. Picking is strictly controlled and when you're offered a homemade bottle of the stuff, it is so nice you can see why!
Kir	an aperitif glass of white wine with a fruit liqueur added – usually cassis (blackcurrant), mûre (blackberry) or framboise (raspberry)
Mutzig	super strong beer and very tasty
Vin chaud	hot mulled wine

Food and drink

Courchevel 1850

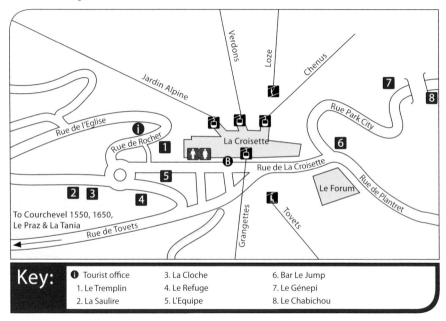

Key:

ℹ Tourist office	3. La Cloche	6. Bar Le Jump
1. Le Tremplin	4. Le Refuge	7. Le Génepi
2. La Saulire	5. L'Equipe	8. Le Chabichou

Courchevel 1650

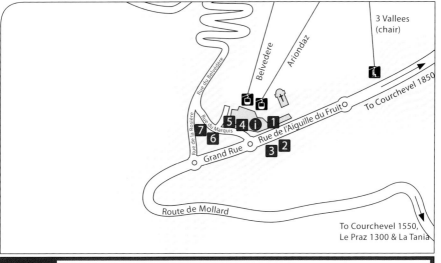

Key:	❶ Tourist office	3. Le Seizena	6. L'Eterlou
	1. Titine et Lilou	4. La Table de Marie	7. Le Petit Savoyard
	2. Rockys	5. Bubble Bar	

Courchevel 1550

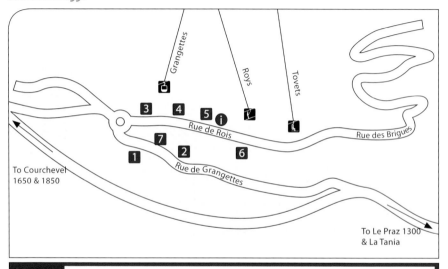

Key:

- ℹ️ Tourist information & ATM
- 1. Le Chanrossa
- 2. La Cortona
- 3. La normandise
- 4. Kikafaim
- 5. Le Caveau
- 6. L'Oeil de Boeuf
- 7. The Bar

Courchevel La Tania

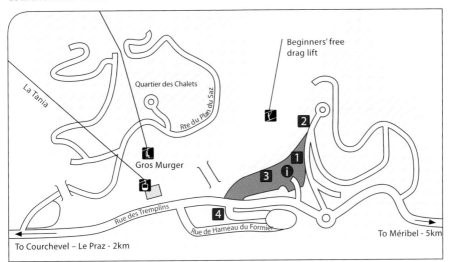

Beginners' free drag lift

Quartier des Chalets

La Tania

Rte du Plan du Saz

Gros Murger

1

2

3

Rue des Tremplins

4

Rue de Hameau du Formier

To Courchevel – Le Praz - 2km

To Méribel - 5km

Key:

- ▨ Main shopping area
- ❶ Tourist office

1. Pub Le Ski Lodge
2. Le Farçon
3. La Ferme de la Tania

4. La Taiga

Courchevel Le Praz

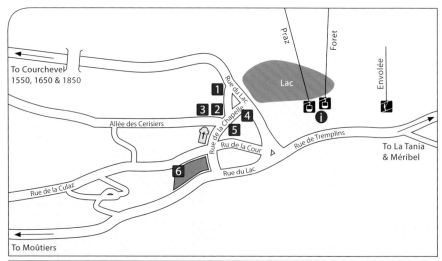

To Courchevel
1550, 1650 & 1850

Praz

Forêt

Lac

Envolée

Rue du Lac

Allée des Cerisiers

Rue de la Chapelle

Ru de la Cour

Rue de Tremplins

To La Tania
& Méribel

Rue du Lac

Rue de la Culaz

To Moûtiers

Key:

Main shopping area
- Tourist information –
  lift pass office, ESF

1. Le Bistrot
2. La Cave d'à Côté
3. Le Ya Ca

4. La Table de mon Grand-Père,
   Les Peupliers Hotel
5. Le Darbeilo

6. L'Escourche-Vel

Our absolute favourites...and why

These are places that our researchers return to time and time again:

La Cloche > 82	Delightful atmosphere and classic French cooking with a gastronomic feel
Le Genépi > 83	Great cooking in a civilized setting run by Thierry and Cecile Mugnier
Bar Le Jump > 84	Lively Brit bar with great après-ski
L'Eterlou > 92	Lovely views and diverse menu
Le Seizena > 85	Great food, beautifully presented and a real change from typical Savoyard cuisine
La Table de Marie > 85	Good value restaurant just minutes from the piste
Chez le Gaulois > 84	Don't miss the incredible reblochon and ham option
L'Oeil de Boeuf > 87	A lovely intimate bar and restaurant, perfect for a romantic meal
La Taiga > 88	A sophisticated setting for après-ski
Pub Le Ski Lodge > 89	Family-friendly by day, loud and live by night
Le Farçon > 89	Gastronomic restaurant right on the piste
Le Darbeilo > 90	Atmospheric, local feel with a classic French menu
Le Bistro du Praz > 90	French gourmet menu complimented by the welcoming service
La Table de mon Grand-Père > 90	Extensive wine list and beautiful food
Le Ya-Ca > 91	Excellent service and food, also very good at meeting dietary requirements

Food and drink

How to read our reviews

Resort restaurants (➤ 82) and bars (➤ 93). Mountain restaurants (➤ 99) are shown by valley.

1850
Le Chabichou
T +33 (0)4 79 08 00 55

Rue des Chenus, 12.30-2pm, 7.30-9.30pm.

This two Michelin star restaurant owned by the Rochedy family is attached to a 4-star hotel. You can eat on the sunny terrace, or inside wearing slippers instead of ski boots. The cannelloni of duck leg in a confit of foie gras comes highly recommended. Evening menus are from €50, €100 and €200.

Reading our reviews:

 Budget: most main course prices are under €10

 Mid-range: main course prices range from €11-20

 Expensive: most main courses are over €20

 Good vegetarian choice

 Our absolute Mad Dog favourites

La Cloche
T +33 (0)4 79 08 31 30

Place du Rocher, 12-12.30pm, 7.30-11pm.

Cosy and intimate, La Cloche offers classic French cuisine with a more elaborate evening menu, as well as an excellent range of regional specialities. Duck fillet roasted with raspberry honey, mashed potatoes and hazelnuts is €29, and medallions of sole, lemon verbena cream and wild rice, €40.

Le Génépi
T +33 (0)4 79 08 08 63

Rue Park City, 12-2.30pm, 7-10.30pm.
Fine French cuisine served by husband and wife, Thierry and Cécile Mugnier. Everything is homemade, including the delicious bread. Try the souris of lamb slow-cooked and served with crozets (€32) or the six course vegetarian menu from €33. Food is complimented by wine personally selected from each region in France by Thierry.

La Saulire
T +33 (0)4 79 08 07 52

Place du Rocher, 12-3pm, 7.30-10pm.
Imaginative menu: roast chicken with wild mushrooms, polenta chips and truffle juice (€35). Two courses from €29, three courses from €40, as well as a dessert menu to die for!

Le Tremplin
T +33 (0)4 79 08 02 33

Place du Tremplin, 8am-12pm, lunch 12-4pm, dinner 8-10.30pm.
Long-established restaurant with an emphasis on fish and shellfish. Lunchtimes offer good, simple food such as pizza and chicken.

If you want something a little more upmarket, ask for the Royal Jumbo Platter with lobster (from €330 for four people). Dinner ranges between €23-45, along with an extensive wine list. Eat in or take-away at the Crêperie next door.

Ten Kai
T +33 (0)4 79 41 18 04

Rue des Tovets.
This great Japanese/sushi bar offers some divine Asian cuisine, worth what you'll be paying, which is between €23-32 for a main course. Assiette Sushi ranges from €7 for five pieces of avocado to €210 for 77 pieces. Take your pick!

Bar Le Jump

T +33 (0)4 79 08 09 00

Place du Forum, 9.30am-1am. Lunch 12-3pm.

Lively Brit bar right by the slopes, and a real institution. A great rendezvous point – if you sit here long enough you'll probably bump into everyone you know in the resort. Après-ski comes with free nibbles served around 5ish and a friendly service. Food is only served at lunchtimes and has a British bias, from between €7.50-14. Children welcome.

Le Refuge

T +33 (0)4 79 08 24 82

Rue Verdons, 9am-2am, food served 12pm-midnight.

Typical French restaurant with a small bar area and wooden tables – a favourite with the locals. You'll feel the sun coming through the large windows, which are also great for people watching. Menu includes steak, fillet of pike perch with leek marmalade and Savoyard specials, ranging from €16-29. Children's menu starts from €9 for one course.

Au Pain D'Antan

Le Forum, 8am-8pm.

Snacks and hot and cold drinks with a small number of tables where you can sit down. Snacks include croque monsieur €3.50, pizza slice €3 and baguettes €4.50-6.

Chez le Gaulois

Le Forum, 9am-8pm.

Freshly squeezed orange juice, baguettes with delicious fillings and pizza slices.

Fast food

On the piste next to Kaliko and opposite the Tovets lift, 12-3pm.
Paninis, sandwiches, chips and kebabs (€3-6).

Sno'limit

T +33 (0)4 79 08 38 44

Rue de Planetrey, 10am-11pm.
Light snacks (€6-10) and drinks.

1650
L'Eterlou

T +33 (0)4 79 08 25 45

Rue de Marquis, 12-2pm, 7-11pm.
Pizzas and pasta at the lower price end of the menu (€8.80-12.50). Savoyard (€15.40-22.20) and French dishes also available. Vegetarians should try the vegetarian tartiflette, €15.60, or cheese fondue for €15.40. Children's menu (under 12s) €9.

Le Seizena

T +33 (0)4 79 08 26 36

8am-11pm.
Great food and beautifully presented – dishes such as roast fillet of duck with honey served with veg and asparagus stir-fry (€17) and sauteed scallops with wok vegetables (€22) make a refreshing change from the usual Savoyard pizza/pasta menus. There is also a good wine selection.

La Table de Marie

T +33 (0)4 79 01 18 97

Rue du Marquis, 8am-midnight.
Great value restaurant just moments from the piste in 1650. Open all day for breakfast, lunch, dinner and take-away pizza (until midnight, €7.10-13.40). Specialities range from bruschetta, all-you-can eat pasta on Sunday night, set price pizzas on Tuesdays and a Tartiflette party on Thursdays for €15.90. Children's menu from €7.60 (two courses).

Food and drink Resort restaurants

Le Petit Savoyard

T +33 (0)4 79 08 27 44

Rue du Marquis, 12-2pm & 7-10.30pm.

An intimate restaurant with skiing memorabilia adorning the walls. Pizzas are excellent (€10.50 – 17.50), but there's also plenty of Savoyard and meat dishes (try the faux filet with morille mushrooms for €28.50) on offer. Vegetarian dishes include the three cheese fondue for €18.50. Children's menu from €13.50 (two courses).

Bubble Bar

T +33 (0)4 79 01 14 21

Rue du Marquis, 8am-1am.

Paninis for €5 for up to four fillings, including real cheddar cheese and Branston pickle – a favourite with season workers missing home comforts. For bar entry see ➤ 97.

Titine & Lilou
(formerly Crêpancakes)

T +33 (0)4 79 08 95 53

On the left towards the end of the first shopping section in 1650, 10am-midnight.

Not only great crêpes (€3-15) but a fantastic breakfast – just the thing for the chalet day off. Cider and beer (€3) and take-away pancakes from €2.50-5.50.

Chez le Gaulois

T +33 (0)4 79 08 31 44

Next to the main bus stop, 7am-7.30pm.

This delicatessen has delicious baguettes for €4.50-6.50. Vegetarians should try the melted raclette (€4.50).

Au Pain D'Antan

Next to the main bus stop, 7am-1.30pm, 3.30-8pm.

Sandwiches €4.50-6.

Rockys

Next to the main bus stop, 9am-midnight.

Think chips (€4), salads (€8) and burger (€10) type menu. Lunch is 12-2.30pm, happy hour 4-6pm and general snacks from 10am-6pm. As well as live music twice a week, Wednesday is theme night and a new weekly comedy night will be starting for the 2007/8 season making it a popular venue. Don't miss out on the hot chocolate (always add marshmallows and cream!) Non-smoking.

1550
Le Caveau
T +33 (0)4 79 08 09 42

Rue des Rois, 12-2.30pm, 7-10.30pm.
If you're looking for a more traditional fondue/raclette sort of joint, Le Caveau is the place for you. As well as feasting on local

cheese dishes, you can choose from a wide variety of Savoyard meat dishes or fill up on the extensive gastronomic menu. Look to pay between €17-29 for your meal, children from €10 (two courses). The vegetarian options are all cheese-based but there is a good variety.

La Cortona
T +33 (0)4 79 08 04 87

Rue des Grangettes, 12-2pm, 7-11pm.
Friendly and reasonably priced pizza/pasta (€8-16) restaurant and a firm favourite with the locals. All the usual Savoyard dishes are available, including a three course menu that comes in at €28. Two courses and a drink for children is

€11. Good vegetarian options on pizza/pasta dishes.

L'Oeil de Boeuf
T +33 (0)4 79 08 22 10

Rue des Rois, 11am-11pm, food served 12-3pm, 7-11pm.
This intimate bar and restaurant is unashamedly aimed at meat lovers. Deer heads adorn the walls and animal skins hang across the seats. Meat dishes are cooked on an open fire and are reasonably priced. Not a huge choice for vegetarians but the Beaufort tart with salad is excellent. Otherwise the Magret du canard with orange (€31) and chicken skewer with lemon and tarragon (€25) are both delicious. Also great for après-ski.

Le Chanrossa
T +33 (0)4 79 08 06 85

*Rue des Grangettes, 7.30-10pm
(for non residents).*
This chalet hotel has started to do
speciality themed meals (Chinese/
curry nights etc), as well as the
usual menu. Try the steak with
Roquefort crushed new potatoes
and mushroom cream sauce (€17)
or the roasted fillet of salmon, new
potatoes and lemon beurre blanc
sauce (€15). Most main courses
range from €15-20. House wines
are €17.50-19 a bottle.

Kikafaim
T +33 (0)4 79 08 54 53

Rue des Rois, 9am-10pm.
A range of sandwiches, paninis
and other snacks, including
excellent kebab (€5.50) and hot
chicken curry sandwich (€5.50).
Pizzas from €10-14 and you can
take your food to eat in La
Taverne bar on the opposite
side of the road.

La Normandise
T +33 (0)4 79 08 16 18

*Underneath the Grangettes lift
building, 8.30am-11pm.*
Crêperie with a deceptively small
entrance; sit down or order from
the take-away window. Sweet and

savoury pancakes (€2.50-10),
tartiflette and salad (€15) and
burgers available. Breakfast on
Saturday is served from 7.30am
and costs €7.50.

The Bar

Rue des Grangettes.
Toasties served 12-4pm – two
fillings for €3. Pie and pint is €6
and a demi is €2 **>** 98.

La Tania
La Taiga
T +33 (0)4 79 08 80 33

*On the road behind the gondola
(opposite the bus stop),
10.30am-1.30am.*
La Taiga provides a more

sophisticated setting for après-ski – leather sofas, stone walls and a fire – as well as being a great place to sample happy hour cocktails (5-7pm). In terms of the food, classic French and Savoyard dishes are on the menu; fresh red tuna steak with bacon sauce (€18) and fillet of venison with red fruit sauce (€20) should all get your taste buds going. Set menus also available.

Pub Le Ski Lodge
T +33 (0)4 79 08 81 49

On the piste at the bottom of Folyères, 10am-2am, food served 12-2.30pm, 7-10pm.
During the day, this legendary

pub is very family-friendly; in the evening, flavoured vodkas, live bands and loud music make it the liveliest place in La Tania. There's a large range of UK-type pub food including burgers (€7-12.50), salads (€6.50-9.50) and a kids menu for €7 (two courses). All major sports fixtures shown. Internet access > 99.

Le Farçon
T +33 (0)4 79 08 80 34

Heading down Folyères, to the left of the piste, 7-10.30pm.
This gastronomic restaurant offers ambitiously complicated dishes but manages to pull it off in spades. Arguably one of the best

restaurants in Courchevel. The beautifully balanced menu offering five cheese-based courses (€45), the nine course degustation menu (€90) and the six course menu including duck fois gras, roast lobster and caramelised scallops (€120) are all exceptional. House wine costs €22. No vegetarian options.

La Ferme de La Tania
T +33 (0)4 79 08 23 25

On the corner, opposite ESF, 10am-11pm.
A great favourite with families and larger groups, especially on chalet staff night off, La Ferme gets booked up quickly. Try the 'chapeau' house speciality – a hot

metal 'hat' which cooks your food in front of you (€23). They also offer the usual Savoyard dishes (€8-23). House wine ranges between €13-15. Take-aways also available.

Le Praz
Le Darbeilo
T +33 (0)4 79 01 11 72

Rue de la Chapelle, 4.45pm-2am.
This restaurant has a huge open fire and a really local feel. Informal yet with an unashamedly French classic menu. The steaks are melt-in-your-mouth fantastic, and other meat dishes are cooked to perfection. Main courses range between €17-26 and a children's menu is available. House wine is

€8.50 for a 50cl pichet or €18.50 for the cheapest bottle.

Le Bistrot du Praz
T +33 (0)4 79 08 41 33

Rue de la Chapelle, 12-2.30pm, 7.30-10.30pm.
French gourmet restaurant with a great menu and really welcoming service. A brother and sister team run the typically Savoyard restaurant – the perfect place for a romantic dinner. Try the tartiflette and green salad (€17) or a main course which range between €22-32.

La Table de mon Grand-Père (Les Peupliers hotel)
T +33 (0)4 79 08 41 42

By the bus stop and facing Olympic Sport, 12-2.30pm, 7-9.30pm.
The majority of the residents of Les Peupliers Hotel eat dinner in the hotel but there are some tables available for non-residents. The food is beautifully presented and the service friendly (most staff speak English). A lunch menu of three courses (€28) and evening menu (€37-46) are available. The usual main courses range from €19-42. Vegetarians should try the homemade tagliatelle with tomato (€14).

La Cave d'à Côté
T +33 (0)4 79 08 42 90

Opposite Les Peupliers Hotel,
midday-9.30pm, food served
12-2.30pm, 7.30-9.30pm.
Owned and run by Les Peupliers
Hotel, this restaurant offers the
usual Savoyard menu and pasta
dishes, as well as daily specials.
You'll be looking to pay between
€14-30 for your main course and
house wine starts at €18 a bottle.
Children welcome.

Le Ya-Ca
T +33 (0)4 79 08 41 04

Rue de la Chapelle, 7.30pm-late.
Only open evenings, this small

tucked away restaurant is a
definite favourite with us. It's
romantic, has excellent food and
service, and is very flexible with
dietary requirements. The three
course menu is €39, with cheaper
main course alternatives ranging
from €29-42. Try the gigot à la
ficelle (€29). Extensive wine list.
Children not allowed.

L'Escourche-Vel
T +33 (0)4 79 08 43 44

Galerie L'Or Blanc,
pub 3.30pm-1.30am,
restaurant 6.30-10.30pm.
Italian restaurant offering a good
choice of pasta dishes (€8-13)
as well as pizzas and other
Italian- style dishes. Savoyard

specialities are on the menu too;
expect to pay between €16.50-30
for a main course. Friendly staff
and children's menu. Compared
with other places in Le Praz, it's
reasonably priced and particularly
popular with families > 19.

Take-aways
1850
Sherpa
Le Forum
> 131. Delivery service. Raclette and fondue equipment rental and take-away fondue and raclette meals.

Le Passage
Le Forum
T +33 (0)4 79 08 20 42

Take-away pizza (€8-15), salads, crêpes, sandwiches (€6-14).

For a real treat, order a take-away from Le Cap Horn
> 106. Delivery is free.
Call +33 (0)6 30 52 84 07
or +33 (0)4 79 08 33 10.

1650
L'Eterlou
> 55. Pizza from €8.50 – buy six pizzas and get the seventh free.

La Ferme des Saveurs
> 132. Small deli which homecooks a different plat du jour each day that you can pre-order. Roast chicken with roast potatoes for 4/5 people costs €22. The usual raclette and fondue can also be ordered.

La Table de Marie
> 85. Take-away pizzas served till midnight (€7.10-13.40).

1550
Sherpa
> 131. Ready roasted chickens available.

La Tania
La Ferme de la Tania
> 89

Snow food
T +33 (0)4 79 08 48 99

The take-away pizzas are delicious. (€7.50-9.50). Sandwiches and paninis also available.

Sherpa
> 132.
Salaisons de 2 Savoie
> 132

Extreme Cuisine
T +33 (0)6 67 92 80 93
W extreme-cuisine.co.uk

If you're bored of doing the Savoyard rounds and are looking for some exotic promise, why now have some Indian cuisine delivered to your door. Main courses are between €8-8.50, and include chicken, prawn or vegetable korma, and tikka masala. Side orders (€1.10-4) include pilau rice, garlic naan and poppadoms with chutney.

Après-ski & nightlife

Courchevel has something for everyone, from upmarket nightclubs and piano bars to noisy live-music venues open till 4am. There is an undeniable British feel to some of the places but in each of the villages you'll find bars where you can soak up some French atmosphere.

Buses run till around midnight (less frequently to and from La Tania) and taxis won't break the bank if you can find someone to share the fare.

Après-ski comes in two categories; the bars you fall into straight off the slopes and the post dinner, late night venues. Many are in both camps but have a slightly different feel later in the evening.

Most bars are quiet during the dinner period of 6.30-9.30pm and will not get going again until after 10pm. This may seem late but it's surprising how energetic you can feel after a couple! Live music venues ➤95.

1850
Bar Le Jump

Right next to La Croisette.

Because of its proximity to pretty much all the ski school meeting points, it can get busy with instructors grabbing a coffee in between lessons. They provide British newspapers you can read if you're waiting for friends. Nibbles served around 5pm to help soak up the après-ski alcohol. Live coverage of all major sports fixtures.

Our favourite bars and nightclubs

Bar Le Jump > 93	Its great location makes it a busy meeting point with a buzzing atmosphere – shuts early
La Bergerie > 95	Originally a sheep shed, now turned bar – popular with the Russian contingent
La Cave d'à Côté > 91	This crêperie does a good trade in après-ski
La Grange > 96	Subterranean restaurant that transforms into a civilised nightclub
Purple Caffé > 97	Guest DJs, go-go and table dancers, speed dating and celeb guests
Piggy's > 96	Great ambience, free nibbles, DJ and live music
Bubble Bar > 97	Themed nights, live music, and the cheapest champagne in Courchevel
L'Oeil de Boeuf > 98	Great for immediate après-ski with a terrace overlooking the pistes in 1550
Taiga > 98	Enjoy happy hour cocktails in comfort
Pub Le Ski Lodge > 99	Loud, lively Brit pub full of UK and antipodeans staff
Les Peupliers > 99	A cosy, quiet place to relax by the fire with a sophisticated drink

L'Aventure

Top level of Le Forum.
Trendy, up-market bar for drinks with a great terrace looking onto the pistes running into 1850.

La Bergerie

T +33 (0)4 79 08 24 70

On the right-hand side of Bellecôte, just above 1850.
Originally a sheep shed (the clue is in the name!), this bar and restaurant is a great place to stop. Although there is a terrace, the rustic interior means it is also a great 'bad weather' day stop. It's an upmarket restaurant in the evening. You can also get to the bar (or back into the resort after a few drinks) via

the road that runs behind it.

Les Bois des Bans

T +33 (0)4 79 08 02 59
Courcheneige Hotel.

Also on Bellecôte on the left as you enter the final tree and chalet-

lined run into Courchevel. Not just a large terrace with a great location, but a cosy lounge where you can sip your hot chocolate or vin chaud by an open fire on colder days.

Live music

Many bars have informal live music occasionally but you'll find more regular entertainment in the following venues:

Le Kalico > 96	Live music Tuesday and Thursday
Le Milk-Pub > 96	Live music or resident DJ most nights
Piggy's > 96	DJ from 8pm and live music from 10pm every night
Bubble bar > 97	Live music twice a week
The Bar > 98	Theme nights and live music through the week
Pub Le Ski Lodge > 99	Twice a week from (Tuesday and Thursday) and sometimes Wednesdays for après-ski
L'Escourche-Vel pub > 91	Live music twice a week – gets busy later on

Les Caves

T +33 (0)4 79 08 12 74

Rue des Tovets, 11pm-4am.
Late night venue, with dark corners, chrome and mirrors. Don't even think about arriving before 11pm. Expensive!

La Grange

T +33 (0)4 79 08 14 61

Rue Park City.
This subterranean restaurant transforms itself into a very civilized nightclub from 11pm till 4am. The setting reflects the restaurant's North African and Moroccan cuisine. Sit at the wooden bar or in the comfortable chairs and imagine yourself in Tangiers.

La Kalico

T +33 (0)4 79 08 20 28

Le Forum.
Breakfast in the morning, on-the-piste busy restaurant by day and club venue by night, with good live music through the week. Open till 4am.

Le Milk-Pub

T +33 (0)4 79 00 48 83
Le Forum, 5pm-2am.
A trendy place for après-ski drinks. Although not massive it's a nice change from the usual wooden interiors you will find in most other places. Live music or a resident DJ most nights and a cool bar to hang out. Access is via a steep staircase so watch your step after you've had a few.

Piggy's

T +33 (0)4 79 08 00 71

Rue de la Croisette, 6pm-2am.
Named after its owner, this 'gothic meets Irish meets Coutts Gold Card' bar is labelled as a pub outside – don't be misled. Settle on the leather sofas and enjoy table service, or sit at the bar with your cocktail. Half a litre of draft Guinness will set you back €12.50, and a cocktail €13 but the ambiance is great and free nibbles are on offer. DJ from 8pm or live music from 10pm

every night. Drink prices increase slightly after 10pm.

Purple Caffé
T +33 (0)4 79 04 06 64

Rue des Tovets, 6pm-2am.
This bar would equally be at home in London or Paris. Walk downstairs over paper rose petals to the intimately lit bar, with discreet corner hideaways. This is a champagne and cocktail bar and the wine list is excellent. Tapas style snacks available. A variety of special events are offered during the week, including guest DJs, go-go and table dancers, speed dating and celebrity guests.

Le Tremplin
Place du Tremplin.
Because of its location and size, this is a busy après-ski spot that's difficult to miss. The large terrace has views of all the pistes that come down into 1850. Try one of the hot rum drinks after a cold day on the mountain. Live music kicks off in the restaurant from 6-8pm and from 9.30pm till closing **>** 95.

1650

Bubble Bar
T +33 (0)4 79 01 14 21

Rue du Marquis, 8am-1am.
Right at the bottom of the pistes in 1650, this bar shows all major sports events and has internet access. They also have live music twice a week. Probably the cheapest champagne in Courchevel at €35 a bottle. Settle into one of the big comfy sofas and read the UK papers. Paninis served from 8am (€5 up to four fillings).

By Night Tavern
L'Ourse Bleue, 5pm-2am.
Enter down a strange red mock-leather padded corridor into a fairly basic bar with TV screens and pool tables.

Moriond Lounge
T +33 (0)4 79 08 23 75

L'Ourse Bleue building, 4pm-4am.
Newish bar run by Aussie Paul
with games room, pool table, big
screen games and live music
through the week. Fantastic
place to hang out with friends
in a lively environment.

1550
L'Oeil de Boeuf
T +33 (0)4 79 08 22 10

Après-ski venue popular with ESF
instructors. The outside terrace
has cosy fur seats with a great
view of the slopes. Not a late night
drinks venue as it becomes a
restaurant in the evening ➤ 87.

La Barouf
T +33 (0)4 79 08 04 71
Rue des Rois, 4pm-2am.
Lively bar with a pub atmosphere
but unlike most 'pubs' in resort,
this one has mainly French
(friendly) staff. A large TV shows
videos and sports but is not too
intrusive.

The Bar
*Rue des Grangettes,
9am-midnight.*
Internet connection (€1 for 15
minutes). Toasties available
(12-4pm). Theme nights and
live music through the week. TV
screen showing all major fixtures
but the bar is tiny so come early to
get a good seat. There is a lock-up
facility for boards outside – ask for
the key that's kept behind the bar.
Five demis (1.25 litres) of Amstel
for €10.

La Tania
La Taiga
*Opposite the bus stop on the road
that runs below La Tania's main
'street'.*
With just one bus an hour, it can
get messy if you miss one (or
two). Enjoy happy hour cocktails
in comfy leather sofas and chairs.
Large TV screen showing music
videos and selected sports. Sunny
terrace in good weather. See
restaurant entry ➤ 88.

Le Pub Ski Lodge

At the bottom of the slopes in La Tania.

Loud, lively Brit pub with mainly UK and antipodean staff. The terrace outside is a great place to catch the last rays and watch everyone skiing home > 89.

Le Praz
Les Peupliers

The bar and terrace of Les Peupliers are on most people's way home making it a natural place for a few beers or a mug of their incredibly potent vin chaud. Later on in the evening, the downstairs bar 'Chez Norbys', is a cosy, quiet place to relax with a fire and comfy sofas, and a nice alternative to the other bars of Le Praz.

L'Escourche-Vel pub

Galerie L'Or Blanc, open till 1.30am.

Not the liveliest place straight after skiing but often packed later on, especially on live music nights. Also known as the sports bar (covering all major events) or the pizzeria by locals.

Mountain restaurants

The piste map can be a confusing thing for hungry skiers. A knife and fork symbol shows you where the restaurants are on the piste but omits anything useful like their names or directions. We have visited all those on the map (plus a few that are handy for the piste but not marked on the official map). Each restaurant shown on our maps on pages 102 – 105 has been allocated a red number so you can easily cross-reference.

In the following pages, you'll find reviews for our favourites places and shorter listings for the others. (Full reviews for all restaurants are on **maddogski.com**).

Almost all piste restaurants have stunning views, so even if we don't recommend their food, they can be great places to have a morning or afternoon break.

If non-skiers can get to a restaurant by foot, we say so. Whilst quite a few of the more remote ones (especially in the other valleys) are inaccessible, you can go quite a long way if you work out your gondolas.

- Courchevel > 106 – 109
- Meribel > 109 – 111
- St Martin > 111 – 112
- Les Menuires > 112 – 115
- Val Thorens > 115 – 117

Almost every restaurant opens and closes with the pistes and lifts. Lunch is generally served from 12-3pm – longer in high season and for self-service restaurants.

If you are set on a particular place, especially if you're part of a larger group, we recommend you book, except in really quiet periods.

For the keen skier, self-service restaurants are a real bonus, especially when it's busy – you can usually be fed and watered in under half an hour. This leaves you free to ski during the quieter lunch period of 12-2pm.

Guide to our symbols > 82.

Mad Dog Ski Courchevel

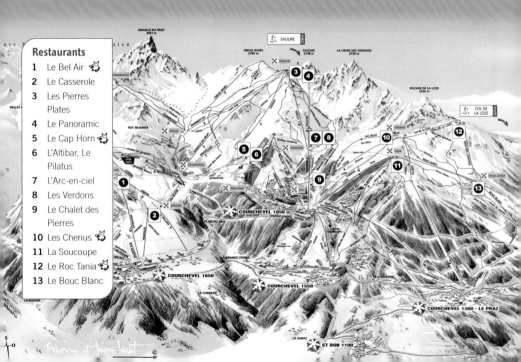

Restaurants

1 Le Bel Air
2 Le Casserole
3 Les Pierres Plates
4 Le Panoramic
5 Le Cap Horn
6 L'Altibar, Le Pilatus
7 L'Arc-en-ciel
8 Les Verdons
9 Le Chalet des Pierres
10 Les Chenus
11 La Soucoupe
12 Le Roc Tania
13 Le Bouc Blanc

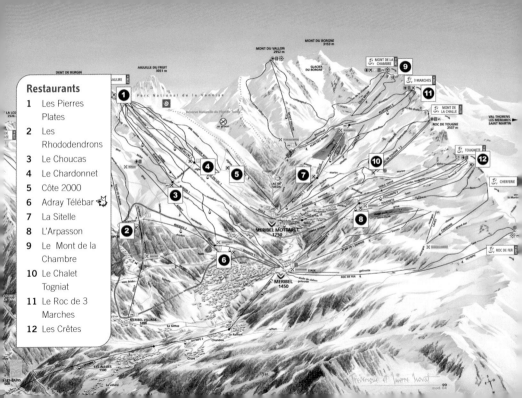

Restaurants

1 Les Pierres Plates
2 Les Rhododendrons
3 Le Choucas
4 Le Chardonnet
5 Côte 2000
6 Adray Télébar
7 La Sitelle
8 L'Arpasson
9 Le Mont de la Chambre
10 Le Chalet Togniat
11 Le Roc de 3 Marches
12 Les Crêtes

Restaurants

1. Le Chardon Bleu
2. Corbeleys
3. La Loy
4. Le Roc de 3 Marches
5. Le Grand Lac
6. Le Chalet des Neiges
7. Chalet du Cairn
8. Mont de la Chambres
9. Les Quatres Vents
10. Le France/Chez Alfred
11. L'Alpage
12. Les Sonnailles
13. Les 3 V
14. Les Roches Blanches
15. Le Panoramic
16. La Ruade

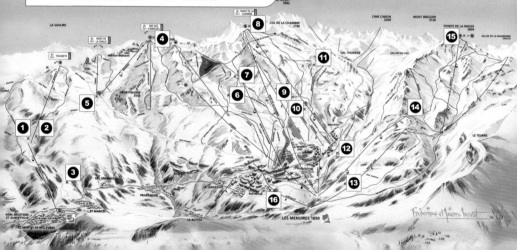

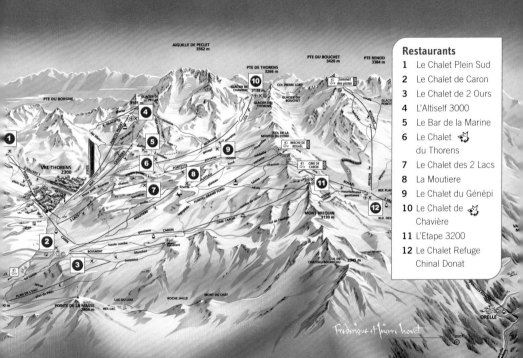

Restaurants

1 Le Chalet Plein Sud
2 Le Chalet de Caron
3 Le Chalet de 2 Ours
4 L'Altiself 3000
5 Le Bar de la Marine
6 Le Chalet du Thorens
7 Le Chalet des 2 Lacs
8 La Moutiere
9 Le Chalet du Génépi
10 Le Chalet de Chavière
11 L'Etape 3200
12 Le Chalet Refuge Chinal Donat

Frédérique et Pierre Novat

Courchevel 1850

L'Altibar, Le Pilatus 6

T +33 (0)4 79 08 20 49

*Pistes: **Pralong**, **Altiport**,
Pedestrian: Altiport shuttle bus.*
Next to the airport, this is
Courchevel's answer to Heathrow's
viewing gallery. Children's menu
available.

L'Arc-en-ciel 7

T +33 (0)4 79 08 38 09

*Pistes: **Combe de Saulire**, **Combe
Pylônes**, **m**, Pedestrian: Verdons.*
Handy watering hole at 1850
mid-station. Friendly service
and consistently good food.
If you pre-book, avoid the
mezzanine floor as it doesn't
have a view.

Le Cap Horn 5

T +33 (0)4 79 08 33 10

*Lifts/Pedestrian: Take the Altiport
lift (shuttle bus for pedestrians) or
head down **Pralong** or **Altiport**.*
The place in Courchevel for an
extravagant lunch. If you can't
stretch to lunch, take a drink stop
to watch the beautiful (and well-
heeled) people of Courchevel.
The famous 'plateau' Cap Horn
(€110 for two) has every shellfish
you can imagine. Or choose an
'appellation controllé' Bresse
chicken (€95). Salads are €17-32
and pasta €23-38.

Careful which wine you
order though; the price list ranges
between €35-13,200. Dining in

the evening by reservation only.
See take-aways **>** 73.

Le Chalet de Pierres 9

T +33 (0)4 79 08 18 61

*Pistes: **Verdons**, Pedestrian: Via G2
Jardin Alpin, requires a short walk.*
Not cheap, but their dessert buffet
is legendary (€16). The side bar
has crêpes and snacks for around
€3-6.

Les Chenus 10

T +33 (0)4 79 08 06 84

*Lifts/Pedestrian: Chenus (with a
short walk uphill), Coqs, Crêtes
then take **Col de la Loze** (requires
a short walk uphill).*
A large and airy restaurant that

gets our vote for being probably the best value self-service in Courchevel, and with a large and sunny terrace. Main courses are between €8.50-21.50, and there's a good choice of snacks, pasta and simple dishes. From here you can ski home to La Tania, Le Praz, 1550 and 1850, making it perfect for the last stop of the day.

Le Panoramic 4
T +33 (0)4 79 08 00 88

Lifts/Pedestrian: Saulire or Burgin-Saulire and Pas du Lac (short walk uphill).
The first floor restaurant serves Savoyard classics along with other less common mountain dishes

such as 'chest of pig' enameled with spices (€25). A more basic self-service is downstairs.

La Soucoupe Restaurant 11
T +33 (0)4 79 08 21 34

*Lifts/Pedestrian: Planetrey, Loze, Bouc Blanc, Chenus (with a 10 minute walk down **Crêtes**, returning the same way) or take **Crêtes** or **Loze Est**.*
The restaurant is a perennial favourite with a cosy wooden chalet feel for colder days or on the fabulously sunny terrace with views of 1850. The delicious food and excellent service contrasts with the quality of food offered in the self-service downstairs,

although the panini and snack bar are good value. Try the grilled lamb chops with thyme (€28) or duck breast in honey (€26).

Les Verdons 8
T +33 (0)4 79 08 38 04

*Lifts: Verdons, Pedestrian: Sources, Rocher de l'Ombre or ski down **Combe de Saulire** or **Combe Pylônes.***
The food is disappointing, staff aren't that friendly and it's not that cheap either – save this one just for drinks breaks. If you want to eat, try l'Arc-en-ciel next door.

Courchevel 1650

Le Bel Air 1
T +33 (0)4 79 08 00 93

Lifts/Pedestrian: Ariondaz (pedestrian), Bel Air or take ***Grandes Bosses***, ***Ariondaz***, ***Pyramide*** *or* ***Rochers*** *– halfway down.*

Fabulous views, three sunny terraces and very friendly (English speaking) service. Food is simple but good quality; roast chicken or pork chops and chips (€17.50). Generally, main courses range between €13.50-31.

In high season they serve a full menu until 3.30pm, but will still offer omelettes, salads and other lighter dishes pretty much until closing time. Booking essential.

La Casserole 2
T: +33 (0)4 79 08 06 35

Lifts: Marquis (with a short walk), 3 Vallées or take ***Grandes Bosses*** *or* ***Ariondaz***.

In direct contrast to its friendly neighbour, Le Bel Air. Although the food is similarly priced, the service is miles apart. If you are planning to eat in 1650, book Le Bel Air.

L'Ours Blanc (not on piste)
T +33 (0)4 79 00 93 93

Situated at the bottom of the runs into 1650.

Typical menu of burgers, pasta, and Savoyard cuisine. No reservations taken.

La Tania

Le Bouc Blanc 13
T +33 (0)4 79 08 80 26

Lifts/Pedestrian: La Tania lift. Alternatively head down ***Dou des Lanches, Jockeys***, ***Lanches, Bouc Blanc*** *or* ***Arolles***.

This is one of the best value mountain restaurants with friendly service, good size portions of tasty food and a handy stop before hitting La Tania. The hot Beaufort tart with salad is excellent (€10). Main courses range between €16-18.20; alternatively try the three course menu for €18. Children welcome (€10 for two courses).

Le Roc Tania 12
T +33 (0)4 79 08 32 34

*Lifts/Pedestrian: **Dou des Lanches**, La Tania, Loze, **Col de la Loze***. Finish a great week's skiing with drinks on this terrace with its amazing views. From here you can ski home pretty much anywhere other than 1650. The menu has all the usual suspects, all well cooked and presented. Options include tagliatelle with Roquefort and walnuts (€13.70) and free range roast chicken (€17.90). They even provide baskets for your gloves, hats and goggles. Children's menu €12.90 (two courses).

Pub Le Ski Lodge (> 89)
Lively restaurant with a sunny terrace serving English pub-type food at the bottom of **Folyères**.

Méribel & Mottaret
Adray Télébar 6
T +33 (0)4 79 08 60 26

*Lifts: Near the bottom of Adret, Rhodos 1 (pedestrians can get there from Meribel - Rond Point 1) or head down **Doron**.*
A much-loved mountain restaurant. It's close to a number of lifts and pistes, so a good meeting place – definitely worth booking ahead. Helpings are generous and menu varied – asparagus with blue cheese, crozets with Reblochon and delicious veal (€12-35). The puddings are highly recommended and chips fantastic. The Télébar is also a lovely place to stop for a jug of vin chaud (€5). You can eat here in the evenings and even book into one of their hotel rooms.

L'Arpasson 8
T +33 (0)4 79 08 54 79

*Lifts: Tougnète 1 or head down **Grive**, **Faon** or **Ecureuil**.*
Good for non-skiers; sunny terrace, friendly staff and quick service. For a longer lunch try the upstairs restaurant.

Food and drink Mountain restaurants

Les Choucas 3

T +33 (0)4 79 00 58 31

*Lifts: Burgin 1 (and a short but quite steep walk down – and back up!) or head down **Cerf**.*

Tucked away below Burgin mid station. Credit cards accepted over €15.

Les Crêtes 12

T +33 (0)4 79 08 56 50,
   +33 (0)6 09 40 51 04

*Lifts: Tougnète 2 (top station) Tougnète Tsk or St Martin 2, then along **Crêtes**.*

A small but very friendly restaurant with amazing views over the Méribel and St Martin valleys.

Les Rhododendrons 2

T +33 (0)4 79 00 50 92

*Lifts: Rhodos 2 or head down **Blanchot**.*

Next to the beginners' area in Méribel and close to the walkers' trails around the Altiport area.

Le Chalet Togniat 10

T +33 (0)4 79 00 45 11

*Lifts: Combes, alternatively ski down **Martre** or **Lagopède**.*

Modern restaurant with an old chalet feel. Self-service and restaurant options. Sunny terrace in the afternoon.

Le Chardonnet 4

T +33 (0)4 79 00 44 81
*Lifts Pas du Lac 1,
or take **Marcassin** or **Niverolle**.*

Great views of the Méribel valley, interesting menu and friendly staff. Worth booking ahead.

Côte 2000 5

T +33 (0)4 79 00 55 40

*Lifts: Ramées from Mottaret or take **Aiglon**.*

A reasonably priced mountain restaurant with most meals under €14. Self-service but your food is brought to your table. Examples of the plat du jour include confit du canard (€15). The restaurant is a lovely place to stop for lunch and one of our favourite places – the staff are always friendly and it has great views and location.

Les Pierres Plates 1
T +33 (0)4 79 00 42 38

Lifts: Burgin 2,
Pas du Lac 2. Also a short ski down from Saulire.
This is in a handy location to meet non-skiers. However, food is average and not cheap.

La Sitelle 7
T +33 (0)4 79 00 43 48

Lifts: Plattières 1 or head down Martre.
This relaxed simple restaurant serves typical Savoyard food but service can be slow on busy days.

Le Blanchot (not on piste)
T +33 (0)4 79 00 55 78

Lifts: Golf (walk goes via Altiport road and also cross-country tracks) or take Blanchot.
Another good place to meet non-skiing friends. Booking essential.

Rond Point (not on piste)
T +33 (0)4 79 00 37 51

Lifts: Rhodos mid-station (alternatively walk from Méribel) or head down Marmotte or Rhodos.
Deservedly one of the most popular bars and restaurants in Méribel, which transforms into a lively après-ski venue with regular live music. The food is a breath of fresh air from the standard Savoyard fare – fish, stir-fry and pasta are all available. Snack bar outside on the terrace and also downstairs sells a range of quick meals and snacks; paninis (€6), chips (€5) and burgers and sandwiches (€8).

St Martin de Belleville
Le Chardon Bleu 1
T +33 (0)4 79 08 95 36

Lifts: Take St Martin 1 and ski down Verdet or Pelozet.
Sunny terrace, good food and reliable service.

Food and drink Mountain restaurants

Le Corbeleys 2
T +33 (0)4 79 08 95 31

*Lifts: Take St Martin 1 and ski down **Verdet** or **Pelozet**.*
Small but relaxed restaurant with a terrace complete with deck chairs for sunny days and limited seating indoors for colder days. Excellent value food although the menu isn't large; typical Savoyard dishes - tartiflette, crozeflette (€9 –15). Wine by the glass starts from €2.20. The dish of the day is usually well worth trying.

La Loy 3
T +33 (0)4 79 08 92 72

*Lifts: Take St Martin 1 and ski down **Biolley**.*
Slightly off the main pistes on the way into St Martin, though still accessible on skis.

La Bouitte (not on piste)
T +33 (0)4 79 08 96 77

St Marcel offers a gastronomic Michelin-starred experience. Reservations essential. They will send a minibus to collect you from St Martin if snow conditions don't allow you to ski there. Don't come here if you are not up for a long lunch (and don't miss the last lifts home!).

Les Menuires

L'Alpage 11
T +33 (0)4 79 00 75 16

*Lifts: Take Montaulever lift and ski down **Mont de la Chambre** or **4 vents**.*
Range of food to suit most tastes and based in a quiet location. Sun terrace for warmer days.

Le Chalet du Cairn 7
T +33 (0)4 79 00 19 81

*Lifts: Take Mont de la Chambre lift and ski down **Liason** or **David Douillet**.*
Large outside terrace for dining on sunny days, as well as deckchairs for a relaxing drink.

Le Chalet des Neiges 6

T +33 (0)4 79 00 60 55

*Lifts: Take the Roc des 3 Marche lift and ski down **Petits Creux** or **Combes**.*

The Chalet des Neiges has excellent, reasonably priced food (main course €8.50-12) in a great atmosphere. Friendly staff offer a quick service complimented by the lovely terrace on which to soak up the sun on lazy afternoons. Kids' menu available.

Les Sonnailles 12

T +33 (0)4 79 00 74 28

*Pistes: **Boulevard Cumin**.*

Sitting with a cluster of other farm buildings on the left as you ski into Les Menuires on the beautiful (and easy) **Boulevard Cumin**. Order at the counter, and your food is then delivered to your table. The menu is good value, and, combined with such a lovely old building, this is a must. Booking is essential (also open most evenings except Sunday and Monday).

La Ruade 16

T +33 (0)4 79 00 63 44

Lifts: Just below Les Menuires – follow signs for Tortollet and Rocher Noir.

Pretty little chalet-type restaurant just below Les Menuires with views up the valley and over La Masse, serving local dishes and a children's menu.

Le France aka Chez Alfred 10

T +33 (0)4 79 00 67 79

*Lifts: Take the Reberty lift and ski down **Boyes** or **Mont de la Chambre**.*

This restaurant needs a bit of TLC but food is cheap and cheerful, with friendly staff and efficient service.

Le Grand Lac 5

T +33 (0)4 79 08 25 78

*Lifts: Ski down the **Gros Tougne** or **Teppes** runs.*

Views up towards Les Menuires valley and down to St Martin. Despite the size, it still manages to feel cosy and authentic. The food is good quality and service is

Food and drink Mountain restaurants

friendly and efficient. Well worth stopping for a nice long, lazy lunch.

Le Mont de la Chambre 8
T +33 (0)4 79 00 67 68

Lifts: Bruyères 2, Mont de la Chambre, Côte Brune.
Self-service is great for a quick, reasonably priced lunch (don't leave without trying the BBQ smelt (€14), it's delicious!). The restaurant is more expensive. Terrace views are mainly blocked by lift buildings.

Le Panoramic 15
T +33 (0)4 79 22 80 60

Lifts: Masse 2.
One of the best views in the Three Valleys, so it's a shame the restaurant isn't better.

Les Quatres Vents 9
T +33 (0)4 79 00 64 44

*Lifts: Take Bruyères 1 and head down **Liaison, Mont de la Chambre** or **4 vents**.*
This restaurant is decked out with very French décor and comes with bags of atmosphere; there's a display of labelled stuffed animals to interest both kids and adults alike, as you don't see much wildlife in the winter. The food is

standard but good and freshly made. Menu isn't large but it has all the usuals. Great terrace for sunny days and large indoor area when the weather's not so nice. Good place to meet non-skiers.

Le Roc des 3 Marches 4
T +33 (0)4 79 00 46 48

Lifts: Allamands, Granges, Plattières 3.
Good meeting point. Limited menu but efficient service.

Les Roches Blanches 14

T +33 (0)4 79 00 60 22

Lifts: Take Masses 1 and ski down **Vallons**.

Good drink stop before you tackle La Masse but prices aren't cheap. Non-customers have to pay to use the toilets.

Les 3 V 13

T +33 (0)4 79 00 60 22

Lifts: **Bd Enverse, Vallons**.

Handy place to stop on the way down Le Masse with views towards Cime de Caron from the terrace.

Val Thorens

L'Altiself 3000 4

T + 33 (0)4 79 00 03 76

Lifts: Take the Funitel or Peclet lift up and ski down **Béranger**. Self-service (€8.60-15) and restaurant (€14-30).

Le Bar de la Marine 5

T + 33 (0)4 79 00 03 12

Lifts: Take the Cascades lift up and come down **Les Dalles** *or* **Tête ronde**.

Upstairs restaurant is more formal and on the expensive side. Downstairs it couldn't be more different; cheap and cheerful with a limited menu.

Le Chalet de 2 Ours 3

T + 33 (0)4 79 01 14 09

Pistes: **Blanchot**.

Nice sun deck for warmer weather. Reasonable vegetarian options and a kids' menu. The interior is filled with bears - hence the name - which will keep the kids amused.

Le Chalet de Caron 2

T + 33 (0)4 79 00 01 71

Lifts: At the bottom of the Boismint, Caron and Mouitiere lifts.
Large restaurant but busy especially on sunny days. Terrace with deckchairs. Children's menu.

Le Chalet de Chavière 10

Lifts: Col.

This tiny mountain refuge at 3120m wins our vote for one of the best views in the Alps, however there has been uncertainty about whether it will re-open this year or not. If you do find it open, there are only two choices on the menu – soup of the day (€7) or a meat, cheese and bread platter (€9). Their small outside area has deckchairs, picnic tables and benches. There are no toilets, and take some cash as credit cards are not accepted.

Le Chalet du Thorens 6

T + 33 (0)4 79 00 02 80

Pistes: 2 Combes, Moraine.

Located at a busy junction with an oversized plastic knife and fork on the roof, this restaurant is difficult to miss. The views are not as good as some of the higher restaurants and the décor isn't brilliant, but it gets our vote for choice and value. Restaurant dishes include fresh pasta and leg of pork with warm lentils (€15). The outside terrace has a cover for colder weather. Downstairs, the self-service café cooks fresh pasta to order and there's also a salad bar. Snacks are available outside for €6-8.

Le Chalet des 2 Lacs 7

T + 33 (0)4 79 00 28 54

Lifts: Les Deux Lacs.

This popular, friendly restaurant gets very busy so be prepared to queue for the outside snack bar if you're in a rush. The restaurant is reasonably priced and the menu offers the usual mountain fair; pastas, tarts, cured meat platters, salads - €9-18. Good sunny terrace and deckchairs. Kids menu available, and a good location for the little ones to ski back into Val Thorens. They don't take reservations so it's best to come early or late.

Le Chalet du Génépi 9

T + 33 (0)4 79 00 03 28

Pistes: Génépi.

Cosy interior which makes it look smaller than it is. Food is simple (pasta, chips etc), and because of the location it can get busy so arriving early is best.

Le Chalet Refuge Chinal Donat 12

T + 33 (0)4 79 56 53 01

Lifts: Take the 3 Vallées express and ski down Gentianes or Combes Roaël/Mauriennaise, Mauriennaise.

The only restaurant in the fourth valley. The menu is nothing special but the food freshly made and quite cheap. Credit cards can be used over €10.

Le Chalet Plein Sud 1

T + 33 (0)4 79 00 04 27

Lifts: Plein Sud.

Standard mountain restaurant menu but cheap prices. Large indoor and outdoor seating areas with good views over Val Thorens.

L'Etape 3200 11

T + 33 (0)6 07 31 04 14

Lifts: Cime Caron cable car.

The highest restaurant in the Three Valleys, with views into the fourth valley and Italy. Unremarkable menu but good quality – we recommend the spaghetti bolognaise. Worth a visit for the views, but avoid the toilets if you can wait!

La Moutiere 8

T + 33 (0)4 79 00 02 67

Lifts: Take the Moutiere lift and ski down Plateau.

Relatively small but homely restaurant. Food is simple but good; ham, egg and chips, chicken and chips etc. Snacks and drinks also available from the window outside.

Are you a Ski Weekender?

The picturesque neighbouring ski resorts of **La Clusaz** and **Le Grand Bornand** are perfect for a long weekend ski break. Just one hour from Geneva airport and with over 220km of varied pistes the skiing is suitable for all levels of skier – from beginners to off–piste experts! NEW for 2008 are 50 snow cannons, re-graded runs and a high-speed lift opening up a whole sector.

Short of time but love to ski? Relax with Ski Weekender!
Offering fully-catered chalet weekend breaks running from Thursday night to Monday evening all through the season, including February, you can choose a time to suit you! Or, if you prefer, take a Ski Midweeker break from Monday night to Thursday evening.

As well as having in-house ski hire and a dedicated instructor, the 4-day Ski Weekender package includes:

• Comfortable ensuite rooms – twin, double or family

• Spacious and well equipped communal chalet areas

• 3 course dinner with wine, breakfast and afternoon tea and cakes

• Lift pass of the whole Aravis region

• Airport transfers to and from Geneva plus inter-resort too

• Services of the friendly ski team, including ski hosting to explore the resort

Prices start from as little as £300 for a 4-day weekend.

For more details call 01202 661 865, email on info@skiweekender.com or go online at www.skiweekender.com

YOUR SKI AND SNOWBOARD WEEKEND AND SHORT BREAK SPECIALIST

SKI WEEKENDER

Can't ski? Won't ski? Too much snow or not enough...? Find out about the host of **other things to do** in Courchevel.

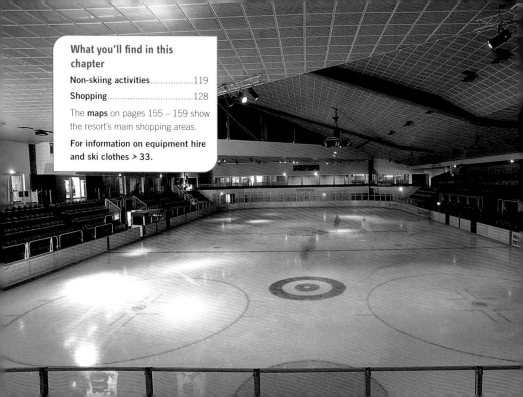

What you'll find in this chapter

The **maps** on pages 155 – 159 show the resort's main shopping areas.

For information on equipment hire and ski clothes > 33.

Life in Courchevel tends to revolve around skiing but if the snow isn't falling, or it's coming down too heavily, there are still plenty of things to do.

If you're not skiing yourself, but are on holiday with people who are, then use the pedestrian access guide for each mountain restaurant (> 99) to work out where to meet your friends for lunch on the mountain.

Beauty, massage and spas
See also Hotel spas and Gyms open to the public.

Pamper Off Piste
T +33 (0)4 79 00 62 56 or
  +33 (0)6 17 60 89 02
W pamperoffpiste.com
A variety of beauty treatments including massages and facials at your chalet, apartment or hotel. Discounts available for multiple, consecutive bookings.

Bowling
T +33 (0)4 79 08 23 83,
Le Forum, 9am-2am every day.
Prices from €7.50-9.50.
Ten pin bowling (booking ahead advised) with a special children's lane (minimum age five). A small café and bar is situated next to the alley serving snacks all day and more substantial dishes at lunchtime and evening. Pool tables and video games available.

Cinema
There are three cinemas in Courchevel:

Cinéma le Tremplin, 1850
T +33 (0)4 79 08 22 39

Cinéma le Terminal, 1850
T +33 (0)4 79 08 00 19

Cinéma le Villard, 1650
T +33 (0)4 79 08 25 01
English films are advertised as 'VOST' (original version with French sub-titles). Programmes are shown on posters throughout the resort and on leaflets in all the tourist offices, or call +33 (0)8 92 68 73 33.

Climbing wall

T +33 (0)4 79 08 19 50
W guides-courchevel.com
Le Forum. Contact the Service des Sports office, 9am-10pm. First climb is €14 (minimum age 5).
Seven routes on a 13m wall. Between 5.30-7.30pm, guides lead you around the rope bridges and a spider's web where you climb to great heights in the Forum shopping centre.

Cookery classes
Le Chabichou Hotel

T +33 (0)4 79 08 00 55
Courses take place on Thursday mornings and there is an option to do an extended course over four mornings (one per week).

Dog-sled rides
Traineau Evasion

T +33 (0)4 79 08 81 55 or
+33 (0)6 68 60 48 24
If you can get to Méribel, you should definitely give the dog-sled ride a try (€55 per person for one hour).

Flights
Aéroclub Dauphiné Courchevel

T +33 (0)4 79 08 31 23
or call Robert Christin on
+33 (0)6 62 24 82 35
Take a tour in a light aircraft around the Three Valleys from €78 per person.

Go-karting on ice
Les Grands Combes

(on the road between 1550 and 1650)
T +33 (0)6 65 51 17 29
E eric.courchevel@free.fr
Ten minutes costs €40 (reservations recommended for groups). See also ice driving and quad biking.

Guided tours

The FACIM (Foundation for International Cultural Actions in the Mountains) organises several guided tours. You can get more information from the tourist office.

SKIPHYSIQUE

LUXURY ALPINE FITNESS SOLUTIONS

We offer a bespoke and fully mobile Physique training service to exclusive guests in Courchevel and Méribel. Qualified personal trainers will visit you in the privacy of your own chalet.

For keen skiers our pre and Apres stretch package will ensure that you get the most out of your time on the mountain.

Whatever your needs, our highly skilled trainers have a treatment to soothe aching limbs and replenish energy levels.

- Yoga
- Pilates
- Boxing
- Tone it up
- Apres Stretch
- Hula
- Swiss Ball
- Physique body and mind
- Jane Fonda workout
- Learn to swim
- Aqua

bookings@skiphysique.com • www.skiphysique.com • UK: +44(0)7920 163 154 • FR: +33 (0)684 373 692

Gym and health clubs

Centre de remise en forme du Forum

T +33 (0)4 79 08 85 54
Le Forum, Monday to Friday 11am-9pm, Sunday 3-9pm. A seven day pass costs €100. You can attend classes or use the cardio gym. They also have a sauna and hamman (steam room)

Hairdressers

See The list, ➤ 150.

Hotel spas and gyms

These are open to the public and most are in 1850.

Diamant Forme
Les Grandes Alpes.
T +33 (0)4 79 08 05 40
Pool, sauna, Jacuzzi, hamman, massages, beauty treatments.

Le Chabichou

T +33 (0)4 79 08 00 55
Beautiful 4-star hotel with spa and beauty facilities open to non-residents. Appointments are required for beauty treatments but you can just turn up for the hamman and sauna (4-8pm, €20). Towels and robes supplied.

Centre Bien Etre des Trois Vallées
Hotel les Trois Vallées
T +33 (0)4 79 08 00 12
Sauna, hamman and range of beauty treatments.

Centre Bien Etre des Neiges
T +33 (0)4 79 08 03 77
Pool, sauna, Jacuzzi, hamman, gym, massages and beauty treatments.

Le Kilimandjaro

T +33 (0)4 79 01 46 46
Massages and beauty treatments are available but it's quite a hike from the centre of 1850.

Les Thermes des Carlina
Hotel Carlina
T +33 (0)4 79 08 00 30
Pool, sauna, Jacuzzi, hamman and beauty treatments.

Le Lana
T +33 (0)4 79 08 01 10
Beauty treatments from Clarins facials to a variety of massages. The spa has a swimming pool, hamman, sauna and Jacuzzi.

La Tania
Hotel Montana
T +33 (0)4 79 08 80 08
5-9pm. €8 per session
Sunbed, very small pool with occasional aqua aerobics sessions, sauna.

Hangliding
Chardon Loisirs
T +33 (0)4 79 08 39 60
E chardonloisirs@wanadoo.fr
€90.
Either from the top of La Loze or the top of Vizelle. Phone first to check weather conditions.

Horse-drawn carriage rides
Place du Tremplin
T +33 (0)6 82 25 64 67 (Maud) or Gérard Chardon on +33 (0)6 08 77 84 72.

15 minute (€25) or 30 minute (€45) rides for up to 4 people.
Take a horse-drawn carriage around 1850. They can also be booked as taxis (prices on request).

Hot air ballooning
Ski Vol Courchevel
T +33 (0)6 83 97 53 26
W skivol.com
Around €220 p.p.

Ice driving
Ecole de pilotage
T +33 (0)6 08 06 67 22
9am-12pm, 4-7pm – weather permitting.
At Le Circuit des Grandes Combes (on route between 1550 and 1650). Reservations essential. If you fancy a ride in a snow

caterpillar, it can be arranged through:

Chardon Loisirs
T +33 (0)4 79 08 39 60
W chardonloisirs.com
€85 for 30 minutes.

Ice skating *(patinoire)*
Le Forum, 1850.
T +33 (0)4 79 08 33 23
3-7pm everyday (2pm during bad weather), 9pm-11pm Wednesday and Friday. €4.80 adult, €3.20 child plus €3.20 for skate hire.
Olympic-size ice rink. Check beforehand as the ice rink closes sometimes for games, shows and training.

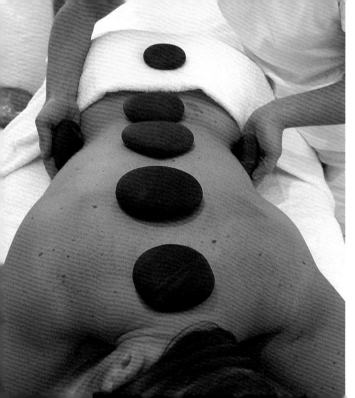

Internet
1850
Cyber Café
T +33 (0)4 79 01 01 01
Rue des Tovets, on the left as you drive into 1850.
French keyboards.

Prends ta luge et tire toi
Le Forum
T +33 (0)4 79 08 78 68
Café, shop and internet access.
French keyboards.

Le Chabichou
Rue des Chenus
T +33 (0)4 79 08 00 55
€4 for 15 minutes, €12 for one hour. Wireless connection available at the same price. No ski boots allowed.

1650
Bubble Bar
UK keyboards (> 97).

Rockys
UK keyboards (> 86).

1550
The Bar
UK keyboards. €1 for 15 minutes. You can also print pages (50c for b/w, €1 for colour) (> 98).

La Tania
Pub Le Ski Lodge
UK keyboards (> 99).

Tourist office
French keyboards.

Le Praz
Tourist office
8.30am-12pm, 2-5.30pm (> 154).

Language classes
La Cité des Langues
Le Forum
T +33 (0)4 79 08 30 40 or
+33 (0)4 79 22 87 66
E tarentaise@lacitedeslangues.com

Luge/Sledging
9am-7.30pm depending on snow conditions (floodlit in the evenings). Free, but you'll need to hire a sledge from one of the larger hire shops – usually around €5.

This luge run is 2km long, with a vertical descent of 300m and an average slope gradient of 15%. You can take the Grangettes gondola back to 1850 (till 7.30pm) or catch the bus from near the bottom of the run.

Massage
See under Beauty, massage and spas and Hotel spas and gyms.

Parapente
Expect to pay around €80 for a tandem flight with a qualified instructor.

Craig's paragliding
T +33 (0)4 79 08 43 65 or
+33 (0)6 81 64 69 70
From Bouc Blanc (at the top of Plantrey and under Crêtes). €90.

Jean-Jacques Dejouy
T +33 (0)6 09 91 13 13

Ski Vol
T +33 (0)6 83 97 53 26
W skivol.com,
From the top of Vizelle and from Col de la Loze.

Air Performance
T +33 (0)6 64 23 90 31

Directicime
FBI (Flying Brigade Instructor)
T +33 (0)6 09 76 50 40
From Col de la Loze.

Tandem Top
T +33 (0)4 79 00 45 67
From Burgin Saulire.

Air Extrême
T +33 (0)6 71 90 21 95

If you're a paraglider already or would like to learn, there are two clubs in Courchevel:

Club des Parapente natur'ailes
Courchevel
T +33 (0)4 79 08 28 87

Delta Parapente club de Courchevel
T +33 (0)4 79 24 04 89

Quad biking on snow
Chardon Loisirs
T +33 (0)4 79 08 39 60
E chardonloisirs@wanadoo.fr
€30 for 12 minutes.

Snow shoeing and hiking
Explore the many footpaths on snow shoes *(raquettes à neige)*, often along breathtaking and silent forest trails. You can join one of the guided tours or book a private guide (see below). The tourist office has a leaflet called *'Snow Shoes and Pedestrian Paths'*, listing walks with and without snow shoes (hire from all good hire shops).

There are 17km of marked groomed trails and 14 separate walking paths.

Courchevel Guides
T +33 (0)6 23 92 46 12
W courchevel-guides.com
€22 per person for a half day, €130 for a private half-day tour.

Raquette Evasion
T +33 (0)4 79 22 04 22 or
   +33 (0)6 80 33 56 11
W raquette-evasion-courchevel.com
€22-25 per person for a half day (plus €5 for equipment). Meeting points throughout the resort.

Yann Couillard
T +33 (0)4 79 01 10 12 or
   +33 (0)6 83 17 78 65
W azimut-rando.fr

€18 for a half day (plus €4 for equipment).

For private tours Yann will come to your accommodation and arrange all the equipment hire. They also offer summer tours.

ESF
1850
T +33 (0)4 79 08 07 72

1650
T +33 (0)4 79 08 26 08

1550
T +33 (0)4 79 08 21 07

Skidoos/Motoneige
Available in 1850 and 1650.
T +33 (0)6 83 97 53 26
W skivol.com
Around €96 solo or €45 behind a guide.

Snow rafting
T +33 (0)4 79 08 39 60
W chardonloisirs.com
Raft down the Olympic ski jump in Le Praz (from around €30 per person).

Squash
Hotel Caravelle
T +33 (0)4 79 08 02 42
10am-10pm. €10-15 per court for 30 minutes.

Swimming
See Gym and health clubs (➤ 122).

Trampolines
La Tania has two big trampolines in front of the tourist office for children from three years old. Wannabe freeriders can practise all their moves before throwing themselves around on the mountain.

Walks

See Snow shoeing **>** 126.

Other events

T +33 (0)4 79 22 01 07

W animationservices.net

T +33 (0)4 79 08 39 60

W chardonloisirs.com

Both companies specialise in
organising bespoke and out of
the ordinary events from torch-lit
descents to skidoo races and
lumberjack evenings!

Shopping

Don't worry about forgetting
essentials as Courchevel has a good
selection of shops, although prices
will usually be more expensive than
the UK. As you would expect, there
is a greater variety of shops in 1850,
but each village has all the basics.

Opening hours

Shops tend to be open from
9am – 7pm often with a break of
two or three hours at lunchtime,
between midday and 2.30pm
(although they usually stay open
all day at weekends and in key
locations near the lifts). Hours vary
depending on weather and busy
periods – if it's essential, phone
ahead to check.

Bakery

1850

Au Pain d'Antan

Rue des Tovets.

T +33 (0)4 79 08 23 07

*7am-1pm, 3.30-8pm and Le
Forum 8am-8pm.*

1650
Boulangerie Gandy
Immeuble le Ceylan
T +33 (0)4 79 08 31 86
7am-2pm, 3-8pm.
Fantastic cakes and pastries.

1550
Au Pain d'Antan
Rue des Grangettes, 7.30am-12.30pm, 4-7.30pm.
Also sells snacks and hot drinks that you can eat inside at one of the small tables.

Le Praz
Le Boulangerie du Praz
T +33 (0)4 79 08 40 33
6.30am-12.30pm, 4-7pm.
Good range of cakes as well as the usual breads.

Pains/Salon du Thé
Galerie de l'Or Blanc, 7.30am-12.30pm, 4.30-7pm.
Bakery with a few tables for hot drinks and cakes.

La Tania
Au Delice de la Source
7am-1pm, 3.30-7pm.
As well as a great range of bread, this boulangerie also sells wine, local honey, beer and tasty patisseries.

Butcher

1850
Boucherie Selva Perrin
Rue du Forum
T +33 (0)4 79 08 20 08
7am-12.30pm, 3-7.30pm (opens 4pm on Sundays and holidays).

Central butcher in 1850 with an appetising range of pre-cooked ready meals that you can buy by weight. A good range of traditional deli food is also available. Located next to the Spar supermarket, so you can conveniently do all your shopping at once. Orders taken by phone, home delivery also available.

1650
Sherpa supermarket
There is a good butcher in the Sherpa, as you enter 1650.

Le Praz
Boucherie Bahler
L'Or Blanc shopping centre.
T +33 (0)4 79 08 41 08
8am-12.20, 3.30-7.15pm.

Off-licence

All the supermarkets listed below sell wine and beers. There are also some specialist shops:

1850

Le Baricou
Rue des Verdons.
T +33 (0)4 79 00 77 72
10am-12pm, 4.30-7.30pm.

Le Chai des Chartrons
T +33 (0)4 79 00 36 53
10.30am-12.30pm, 4.30-8pm (closed Sunday morning).

Le Praz
Cooperative Laiterie
Rue de la Chappelle.
T +33 (0)4 79 08 03 61
9.30am-12.15pm, 3.30-7.30pm, Sunday-Thursday, 8.30-12.15, 3.15-7.30pm, Friday-Saturday.

Ski clothing and equipment
➤ 33.

Supermarkets and delicatessens

There are plenty of supermarkets throughout Courchevel. Hours are usually 8.30am-1pm, 4-7.30pm. Some offer a home delivery service (approx €8 or free for orders over €100). It's worth bringing some essentials with you (teabags, marmite etc), as resort prices can be astronomical.

Sherpa supermarkets also offer a pre-ordering system on www.sherpa.net although you might find it difficult to use if you don't speak French reasonably well.

Moûtiers

There is a Hyper Champion on the left as you drive into Moûtiers from Albertville. Super U is smaller but easier to find on the right as you leave Moûtiers, driving towards Méribel and Courchevel. There's also a Lidl and a supermarket called Ataq, which are cheaper than the other supermarkets but sometimes lacks the basics.

1850

Spar
Rue des Tovets.
T +33 (0)4 79 08 04 40
9am-12.30pm, 3.30-7.30pm.
This is the largest supermarket in the resort. Delivery service available.

Sherpa
Le Forum.
T +33 (0)4 79 08 40 39
8.30am-12.30pm, 3.30-7.30pm.
Delivery service available. Raclette and fondue equipment rental and ready to take-away fondue and raclette meals.

Chez le Gaulois
Le Forum.
T +33 (0)4 79 08 03 99
9am-8pm.
Great little deli, on the top street level of Le Forum. Sandwiches and snacks at lunchtime, take-away raclette also available.

Chez Ma Cousine
Rue de la Croisette.
T + 33 (0)4 79 08 21 68
9am-12.30pm, 3-7.30pm.
Good selection of cheese, wine and cured meats.

1650
Two Sherpa supermarkets – both on the main road and both offering home delivery, roast chickens, take-away raclette and fondue. L'Ourse Bleue also has take-away pizzas.

L'Ourse Bleue
Top of 1650.
T +33 (0)4 79 08 20 33
8am-12.30pm, 3.30-8pm.

Moriond
T +33 (0)4 79 08 11 51
8.30am-1pm, 4-7.30pm.

Spar
Rue du Marquis.
T +33 (0)4 79 08 18 79
7.30am-9pm, 7 days a week.

1550
Sherpa
Rue des Grangettes.
T +33 (0)4 79 08 28 78
8.30am-12.30pm, 4-7.45pm.
As well as ready roasted chickens, you can buy take-away raclette, fondue and pierre chaud for €9.90. The hire of the raclette machine is included in the price.

Chez le Gaulois
Immeuble le Ceylan.
T +33 (0)4 79 08 31 44
Great deli with sandwiches and snacks at lunchtime. Raclette to take-away.

La Ferme des Saveurs
T +33 (0)4 79 08 95 38
8am-1pm, 3-8pm.
Deli stocking a good mix of cheese, wine, charcuterie (cooked meats), prepared meals and tinned food. A different dish of the day, every day, which can be pre-ordered, as well as ready roasted chickens, raclette and fondue take-aways.

Le Praz
Sherpa
Rue de la Cour.
8am-12.30pm, 3.30-7.30pm.
On Fridays there is 10% off the local cheese, ham and wine.

Boucherie Bahler
See Butchers > 129.

Cooperative Laiterie
Rue de la Chappelle.
T +33 (0)4 79 24 03 65
9am-12.15pm, 3.30-7pm.
Good range of wines and local cheeses and meats. Also sells bread, milk and eggs.

La Tania
Sherpa
Behind the Pub Ski Lodge.
T +33 (0)4 79 08 80 69
8am-1pm, 4-7.30pm.
Take-away raclette and fondue. Telephone orders accepted. See also Take-aways > 73.

Salaisons de 2 Savoie
8am-8pm.
Small delicatessen next to L'Arbatte bar. They stock a good range of local produce from honey to 'diots'

(local sausages). Roast chickens are €9.50 and take-away lunch is €7 for a sandwich, dessert and drink.

Newsagents and tobacconists
1850
Maison de la press
Le Forum.
T: +33 (0)4 79 08 16 01
8am-8pm.
Photocopying and fax service.

Bureau de tabac
Rue de Plantret.
8.30am-7.15pm.

1650
Snow Press
T: +33 (0)4 79 08 27 64
8.30am-12.30pm, 3-7.30pm.

Tabac les Marmottes
8am-12.30pm, 2-8pm.
Tobacconists only (no papers).

1550
La Boule de Neige
Rue des Rois, Monday to Friday: 8.30am-12.30pm, 2.30-7.30pm (sometimes 3.30pm on sunny days!), Saturday to Sunday: 8.30am-7.30pm.
Newspapers, magazines, t-shirts, gifts, toys and fireworks.

Le Praz
La Presse
8.30am-12.30pm, 2.30-7pm.

Pharmacy
1850
Peizerat Marie-Francoise
Rue de Rocher.
T +33 (0)4 79 08 05 37
9am-7.30pm.

1650
Fabienne and Xavier Duitoux
9am-7pm everyday.

Photography
1850
Cristo Photo
Rue de Rocher.
T +33 (0)4 79 08 25 51
9.30am-7.30pm.

Yavaz Photo
Le Forum.
9.30am-1pm, 2.30-7.30pm.
A second shop is in the Espace Diamant. One hour film processing.

Jean Pierre Photography
Rue des Tovets.
T +33 (0)4 79 08 23 32 *10.30am-12.30pm, 3-8pm.*

Imag'in
Rue de la Croisette.
T +33 (0)4 79 00 19 10
10am-1pm, 3.-7.30pm.

1650
Olivier Photo
Rue de Marquis.
T +33 (0)6 11 42 44 55

Le Praz
Jean-Christopher Photo
Rue de la Chapelle.
T +33 (0)4 79 00 17 11
Book a professional video cameraman to video you when you are skiing.

Animation services
T +33 (0)4 79 22 01 08
W www.animationservices.net

Buffalo Bull's Back Fat

Le Chef Omaha

Skiing with **children**... dream or nightmare? With a little planning, it can be your best ski holiday ever.

What you'll find in this chapter

Skiing can be a fantastic family holiday and Courchevel has a lot to offer for children.

Courchevel is a member of 'Les p'tits Montagnards' club set up by Ski France to recognise child-friendly resorts. This takes into account areas such as medical facilities to child friendly restaurants. **> maddogski.com**.

Accommodation

Children love the social interaction of chalets and hotels and childcare costs can usually be shared and are simpler to arrange, especially through tour operators. On the other hand, self-catering arrangements are more flexible (particularly at meal times).

If you have young children, being close to the slopes, a bus stop or a ski locker is particularly important, as you will inevitably end up carrying their skis as well as your own!

Accommodation checklist

There are a number of questions you may want to ask when booking your holiday:

- Are there price reductions for children?
- Are cots, high chairs and baby monitors provided (or can they be hired)?
- Can extra beds be added into the parents' room?
- Are any other children booked into the chalet? How old are they?
- Are the children's rooms located away from the communal area (which can be noisy until late)?
- Are there baths available rather than just showers?
- Can the company provide nannies and/or babysitters or recommend someone local? What qualifications do they have and what is the adult to child ratio?
- Can high tea be arranged for the children?
- Is it a long or uphill walk to the slopes/nearest bus stop? If so, does the company provide a shuttle bus or lockers near the slopes?

Child-friendly tour operators

Although many chalets and some hotels offer childcare, demand is usually high, especially in school holiday periods, so make sure you book as early as possible.

The companies listed here have a great reputation for being family friendly.

Mark Warner

T +44 (0)871 703 3888
W markwarner.co.uk

Mark Warner's level of repeat business is testament to their commitment to families holidaying in the Alps. Clubs are run by trained nannies for children from four months and upwards.

Crystal

T +44 (0)870 160 4070
W crystalski.co.uk

Crystal offer a wide range of accommodation, some with family rooms and free child places.

Inghams

T +44 (0)20 8780 8810
W inghams.co.uk

Inghams offer chalets, hotels and apartments throughout Courchevel. Children under 18 months have free ski and boot hire when two adults pre-book their equipment hire through Inghams.

Scott Dunn

T +44 (0)208 682 5050
W scottdunn.com

Luxury holidays, offering nannies, children's club and ski school.

Thoughtful additions such as buying your baby's nappies make your holiday easier. They also give you an end of day report on your child's activities.

Le Ski

T +44 (0)1484 548996
W leski.com

Five chalets in La Tania with two crèches. Childcare is offered six days a week (six months to 12 years). Their lunch supervision fits in with ski schools. The 1650 accommodation doesn't have a crèche but they can put you in touch with local childcare companies.

Snowline

T +44 (0)844 557 1323
W snowline.co.uk
Private nanny service in La Tania.

Supertravel

T +44 (0)207 295 1650
W supertravel.co.uk
Supertravel's chalets are in 1850. Their resort staff will drive your young ones to and from ski school. Nannies five days a week.

Family Friendly Skiing

T +44 (0)161 764 4520 (UK) or
+33 (0)4 50 32 71 21 (France)
W familyfriendlyskiing.com
Tony and Julie McMahon have been offering family focused holidays for over 10 seasons. Their Polar Bear Fun Club offers childcare five half days a week, as well as babysitting some evenings and free childcare on selected weeks. Based in La Tania and Le Praz.

Ski Esprit

T +44 (0)1252 618 300
W esprit-holidays.co.uk
The Esprit childcare team are a familiar site in Le Praz as they shepherd their charges around the village. Childcare options depending on age.

Ski Beat

T +44 (0)1243 780 405
W skibeat.co.uk
Based in La Tania, they offer a private nanny service, crèche and a ski school/afternoon option where the nannies will collect your children from the ski school. The crèche is based in Chalets Amethyste 1 & 2.

Skivolution

T +44 (0)1635 37774 (UK)
+33 (0)6 12 52 82 29 (France)
W skivolution.co.uk

Lift passes

Make the most of the Family Pass, with significant discounts on a six to 21 day holiday (minimum of four people; two adults and at least two children under 18).

Children under five have free lift passes (with proof of age and a photograph).

Childcare

If your accommodation owner cannot help you, try:

La Tania

For children from three years old, La Tania has a children's play area, 'La Maison des Enfants', which offers both indoor and outdoor games. This can be booked though the tourist office: **T** +33 (0)4 79 08 40 40.

Kindergardens in 1850 and 1650 are also available from ESF (Ecole du Ski Français) > 32.

Whilst your chalet host might offer babysitting (also check notice boards in local bars and tourist offices) they may not be qualified.

Ski school

Generally, children can start skiing from around the age of four and this is the earliest most schools will accept them. The stronger their leg muscles are, the easier they will find snow ploughs and the more fun they will have. Very young children (up to six) may only have the energy to do half a day on the slopes. The rest of the time might be better spent playing in the snow, or back in the resort (suggested activities > 141).

If your kids have fun they'll be hooked for life and the technical improvement will come so don't worry too much about monitoring progress.

Group or private lessons

British ski schools tend to offer smaller groups, where your kids can benefit from the social side of being in a class and the friendly interaction with other children makes this an ideal environment in which to learn. If you book ESF remember to request an English-speaking instructor. If you're taking lessons too, check that your meeting point is close to your children's for dropping them off and collecting them.

**ESF Kindergarten
1850**
T +33 (0)4 79 08 08 47
W esfcourchevel.com

1650

T +33 (0)4 79 08 26 08
W esfcourchevel1650.com

La Tania

T +33 (0)4 79 08 80 39
W esf-latania.com

Well-equipped facilities accommodate children from the age of 18 months under the supervision of professionally trained child carers. Includes indoor games and outdoor activities.

1550

ESF Village des enfants

T +33 (0)4 79 08 21 07
Club D'Oursons

La Tania

T +33 (0)4 79 08 80 39
Club des Piou Piou
French ski school, minimum age three (four in La Tania), Sunday or Monday start usually available, all have a moving carpet. ➤ 32.

Magic Academy

1850

T +33 (0)4 79 08 11 99
W magic-courchevel.com

La Tania

T +33 (0)4 79 01 07 85
W magic-latania.com
International ski school, minimum age four, maximum group size six. Sunday and Monday starts usually available.

New Generation

T +33 (0)4 79 01 03 18
W skinewgen.com
Minimum age four, Sunday or Monday start, maximum group size eight (six for four and five year olds). Helper in some classes. Full morning lessons for six-12 year olds ➤ 32.

Supreme Ski

T +44 (01479 810 800 (UK) or +33 (0)4 79 08 27 87 (France)
W supremeski.com
Minimum age six, Sunday or Monday start, maximum group size eight (six for four and five year olds). Helper in some classes. Race camp (maximum group eight) for nine-14 year olds ➤ 33.

First day at ski school

- Write your contact number on a piece of paper and put it in your child's pocket
- Plenty of sun cream (water resistant and at least 30 SPF) is essential. Put the tube in their pocket so they can top up throughout the day
- Most schools insist that children wear ski helmets. You can hire these in resort
- Younger eyes are more sensitive so good sunglasses or goggles are important. If you only buy one, goggles are more versatile and less easy to lose
- Choose gloves or mittens your child can take on and off easily themselves; they'll have to do this numerous times throughout the day. (If possible, choose ones that attach to their clothing)
- Slightly older kids can use a small rucksack for carrying drinks, snacks and sun cream. Make sure they are careful not to catch them on chairlifts though
- Children lose body heat faster than adults so make sure they're wrapped up warmly
- If you're booking younger children into ski school, remember to give them a drink and snack for the mid-lesson break
- Even if your children are not in ski school, use sticky labels or band-aids to mark skis and helmets with their name as things are often thrown into a big bundle
- Complete beginners (especially little ones) will not need poles in ski lessons, at least at first
- Check if they need a lift pass or if it is included in the cost of lessons

Children's activities

These suggestions are particularly good for kids but also see **Other things to do** > 119.

Bowling

The bowling alley in 1850 has special children's lanes and can be pre-booked > 119.

Horse-drawn carriage rides
> 123.

Ice skating
> 123.

Indian tee-pee

During school holidays there's usually a tipi on the slopes where kids can have a go with a bow and arrow, and learn about Native American traditions. Check with the tourist office.

Liane di Tarzan

T +33 (0)4 79 01 03 66
Every day from 5.30-7.30pm, €7. Information and booking from the Mountain Guides' office in Le Forum.
A Tarzan rope and assault course in Le Forum.

Playgrounds

Small play area in Le Praz next to the lift building.

Sledging

Buy sledges and bum boards from most shops and supermarkets. Older children can take the luge run > 125.

Swimming

> 122 for hotel pools in Courchevel, or if you have a car you can drive to the public swimming pool in Méribel.

Tobogganing

> 125.

Shopping

Most supermarkets stock babyfood and formula but if you have any favourite products, it's best to bring them with you. Most ski shops have children's sizes too so it's easy to replace any lost items. For toys try tabacs, the many gift shops and Le Pays des Joyets in 1850 on the cut through between Rue de la Croisette and Rue des Verdons.

Restaurants

Restaurants in resort and on the mountain usually go out of their way to welcome children. Most offer simple dishes and some have children's menus or portions. We particularly like these places.

In resort

Bar Le Jump (lunch only)
> 84.

La Table de Marie
> 85.

Pub Le Ski Lodge
> 89.

L'Escourche-Vel
> 91.

Mountain restaurants

The main problem on the mountain is the lunchtime queue. To avoid this, reserve a table or eat early (before 12.30pm). Service is usually quicker at self-service restaurants, or pack your own lunch and enjoy a panoramic picnic ➤ 73.

These are our favourites for families (other mountain restaurants ➤ 99).

Les Chenus
➤ 106.

Le Bel Air
➤ 108.

Le Roc Tania
➤ 109.

Les Rhododendrons
➤ 110.

Le Grand Lac
➤ 113.

COURCHEVEL

SAVOIE - FRANCE

The list – it might sound boring but you'll find all the important information that you don't know you need till you need it...

Telephones

- Telephone numbers include the international dialling code 00 33 (referred to as +33 throughout this book). From Courchevel, drop the '+33' and then dial the number using the (0). For example, if dialling +33 (0)8 20 32 03 68, you would simply dial 08 20 32 03 68

- French numbers beginning with '06' are mobile telephones

Banks, bureau de change and cashpoints

The only banks are in 1850, in or close to La Croisette although you'll find cashpoints throughout the resort. All banks are shut at weekends, except Crédit Agricole.

Banque Populaire
Rue de Plantrey, opposite the entrance to Le Forum, 8.30am-12.15pm, 2.35-6.15pm.

Banque de Savoie
La Croisette, 8.50am-12pm, 1.40-5.30pm (Monday to Thursday), 8.50am-12pm, 1.40-4.20pm (Friday).
Also a bureau de change.

CIC Lyonnaise de Banque
La Croisette, 9am-12.45pm, 2.30-6pm.

Crédit Agricole
La Croisette, 8.30am-midday, 1.45-6pm Monday to Friday, *8.30am-12.10pm Saturday.*

Moûtiers also has several banks.

Cashpoints

1850
La Croisette and Le Forum.

1650
By the bus stop.

1550
In the tourist office.

Le Praz
Next to the bus stop at Les Peupliers Hotel.

La Tania
Next to the tourist office and post office.

Buses

Free shuttle buses run at half hour intervals all day, making it easy to get between all the Courchevel villages. They run more frequently between 1650 and 1850 and less frequently to La Tania. Look for the 'Arrêt Navette' or 'Arrêt Bus' signs and remember to wait on the correct side of the road!

There are also free buses up to the satellite areas (Brigues in 1550, Bellecôte in 1650, and Altiport and Jardin Alpin in 1850). At less frequent intervals, the buses also run to Bozel and St.Bon, the two villages further down.

The bus schedule is less frequent at the very beginning and end of the season. Timetables are shown at each bus stop and you can get your own copy from the tourist office.

Public buses (not free) also run to Moûtiers and on to Chambéry, Lyon and Geneva.

T +33 (0)8 20 32 03 68
W altibus.com

Car Hire

For information on car hire from airports **>** 18. If you want to hire a car in resort, it's worth making your reservation well in advance.

Car parks

If you don't have parking at your chalet or hotel, there are public car parks in each village but they're not cheap.

1850 has a number of car parks. Check with your accommodation which is closest. The most central is covered parking in La Croisette (320 spaces). First hour free. €70 for seven days.

1650 Cimes Blanche

(460 spaces). Turn left (almost back on yourself) at the second roundabout as you drive up the hill into 1650. The covered car park is on your right. First hour free. €60 for seven days.

1550 Grangettes

(170 spaces). La Grangettes gondola. First hour free. €60 for seven days.

Le Praz Jean Blanc

(250 spaces). On your left as you leave the village going up the hill. Uncovered. Free.

Le Tania

There are two free uncovered car parks; parking du Saz and parking du Formier.

Underground parking can be arranged through the tourist office. €60 for seven days.

Cashpoints

See Banks, bureau de change and cashpoints.

Chiropodist

Bernard Leboucq
(1850)
T +33 (0)4 79 08 21 19

Churches

There are churches in 1850, 1650, 1550 and Le Praz. Service times are displayed on notice boards or at the tourist offices.

Credit cards

Although payment by credit card is commonplace, many French establishments (especially restaurants) do not accept American Express.

You will need to have a PIN number to use both credit and debit cards in France.

Dentist
Phillippe Dominique
(1850).
Centre medical du forum.
T +33 (0)4 79 08 19 41

Doctor
The tourist office has a list of duty doctors. Outside opening hours, dial 15 for emergencies.

1850:
9-1pm, 3-7pm.

Marc Chedal
T +33 (0)4 79 08 20 14

Eric Chorlay
T +33 (0)4 79 08 26 40

Bernard Pepin
T +33 (0)4 79 08 20 03

1650
Andène Maalej
T +33 (0)4 79 08 04 45
10am-6pm.

Moûtiers
Moûtiers Hospital
T +33 (0)4 79 09 60 60

Le Praz
Dr Noblins
T +33 (0)4 79 08 43 24
Dr Noblins spent some time practising in London and speaks excellent English.

Dry cleaning
1850
Le Forum.
Level 2, 8am-10pm.
Service washes available
9am-5pm.

1650
Blanchisserie de Moriond
Just above the bus stop.
T +33 (0)4 79 08 22 54
9am-12.30pm, 2.30-7pm.
They also offer a bed linen cleaning service.
1550
Des Neiges et du Soleil
Grangettes building, Rue des Rois.
T +33 (0)4 79 08 03 20
9.30am-12.30pm, 2.30-7pm,
Monday-Saturday.
Dry cleaning and washing. You put the wash on yourself and the attendant will dry it and leave it in

a laundry basket for you to collect later. 5kg/7kg washed and dried for €9/12.

Le Praz
Galerie de L'Or Blanc
T +33 (0)4 79 01 17 76
Launderette open 7am-10pm everyday. Service washes 9am-12pm, 2-6pm (Monday-Saturday), 10am-12pm,3-6pm (Sunday).

Electricity
France operates on 220v but most UK appliances should work with an adaptor (the two round pin type).

Emergency numbers
Air glacier heli ambulance (for major accidents such as avalanches):

Fire brigade: 18

Medical emergency: 15

Piste emergency:
- Courchevel 1850/1650/1550/ Le Praz/La Tania:
  +33 (0)4 79 08 99 00
- Méribel – Mottaret:
  +33 (0)4 79 00 43 44
- Méribel:
  +33 (0)4 79 08 65 32
- Les Menuires/St Martin:
  +33 (0)4 79 00 64 47
- Val Thorens:
  +33 (0)4 79 00 01 80
- Orelle:
  +33 (0)4 79 56 88 01

Police: 17
Local police:
+33 (0)4 79 08 45 03

Garages

1850

Georges Herpin
Place du Forum.
T +33 (0)4 79 08 05 25

1650
Garage/Station du Moriond
T +33 (0)4 79 08 27 52

Moûtiers

These tend to be cheaper than the garages in resort:

Maxauto
166 Allée des Pins in Moûtiers' commercial district.
T +33 (0)4 79 24 40 20
Friendly service and they speak reasonable English.

Euromaster
80 Faubourg de la Madeleine.
T +33 (0)4 79 24 21 95

The environment

There's always a tremendous amount of rubbish on the slopes when the snow melts – don't add to it! A single cigarette butt contains 4,000 toxic substances and can pollute up to 1.3m of snow – under any one chairlift there could be up to 30,000 butts.

How long does rubbish last?

Plastic bottle: 100-1000 years
Aluminium cans: 100-500 years
Cigarette stubs: 2-7 years
Fruit peel: 3 days – 6 months
Sweet wrappers: 100-450 years

Source: www.mountain-riders.org

The Ski Club of Great Britain runs a **Respect the Mountain** campaign to safeguard the environment and the long-term future of skiing. www.respectthemountain.com

Hairdresser
1850

Coiffure Diamant
T +33 (0)4 79 08 39 95

Leist'n Hair Coiffure
In Hotel Carlina
T +33 (0)4 79 08 46 30

Hotel Bellecôte
T +33 (0)4 79 08 11 15

Health
A few tips to keep you healthy on holiday:

- The sun is much stronger at altitude – make sure you wear sun cream, even on overcast days.
- You need to drink at least three times as much water to keep hydrated at altitude – more if you're topping up with wine and beer! Your muscles are the first part of your body to dehydrate so

Useful phrases:	
Hello	Bonjour
Goodbye	Au revoir
How are you?	Comment ça va?
Please	S'il vous plait
Thank-you	Merci
Excuse me/sorry	Excusez-moi
How much...?	C'est combien?
The bill please	L'addition, s'il vous plait
Jug of tap water	Un carafe d'eau
Snowboard	Snowboard
Skis	Les skis
Ski/boarding boots	Chaussures des ski/surf ski/ boarding boots
Ski poles	Batons
Lift pass	Forfait
I am lost	Je suis perdu
Where is the nearest lift/ restaurant?	Ou est le télésiège/restaurant le plus près?
Help!	Au secours!
Watch out!	Attention!

you'll suffer less aches and pains if you keep hydrated.

- Good sunglasses are a must to prevent watering eyes and snow blindness.
- Lip salves with a high sun-protection factor will prevent unattractive chapped lips!

Hospital

The nearest hospital is in Moûtiers.
T +33 (0)4 79 09 60 60

Internet

> 124.

Language

Although many of the people working in shops and restaurants speak English, a little French goes a long way. See our list of useful phrases opposite.

Massages

> 119.

Money

Prices in this book are given in euro (€) unless indicated otherwise. You can find the up-to-date exchange rate at **xe.com**. Cashpoints (> 145), Credit cards (> 146).

Physiotherapist

1850, Rue de la Croisette
T +33 (0) 6 68 57 00 99
British chartered physiotherapy clinic.

Police

The local police can be contacted on:

T +33 (0)4 79 08 34 69

Post Office

Post boxes are small, yellow and usually fixed to the wall.

1850

La Croisette

T +33 (0)4 79 08 06 49
8.30am-1pm, 3-6pm (closes 5.15 on Friday), 8.30am-12pm on Saturday.

1650

By the bus stop heading down the hill

T: +33 (0)4 79 08 27 80
9am-12.30pm, closed weekends.

Le Praz

Galerie L'Or Blanc

T +33 (0)4 79 08 41 03
9.30am-12.30pm, 3-5.30pm Monday – Friday. Closed weekends.

La Tania

Next to the tourist office

T +33 (0)4 79 08 40 40
2.30-6.30pm.

Radio

Radio Nostalgie Courchevel (93.2fm) and Radio R' Méribel (97.9 and 98.9fm) are the local radio stations. The latter broadcasts English information (news and forecasts) between 8-9am and after 6pm.

Safety

Ski resorts are traditionally a safe place to holiday. Most crime involves theft so ensure you keep your belongings with you in the bar and also keep your accommodation locked at all times.

To protect your skis from thieves, you should get into the habit of swapping skis with your companions so you leave mismatched pairs outside restaurants and bars or use a ski padlock which you can pick up for around €10-15.

Resort updates

maddogski.com has snow reports, weather forecasts and webcams for Courchevel. You can also sign up for our regular newsletter.

Taxis

Taxis aren't cheap (particularly at night) but they are an easy way to get around, especially if there's a group of you (expect to pay about €20 from 1850 to Le Praz). There are several local taxi companies all of whom speak English, or restaurants can call one for you.

Altitud'taxi
T +33 (0)4 79 08 15 15
E altitud@taxis2savoie.com

Arolle Taxi
T +33 (0)4 79 01 09 99
+33 (0)6 12 28 59 05
E jean-hubert.melin@manadoo.fr

Blanc Le Praz
T +33 (0)4 79 08 41 10

Christian Ginet
T +33 (0)4 79 08 02 92
E taxis-ecureuil@wanadoo.fr

Locotax
T +33 (0)4 79 01 10 10
E info@locatax.com
Cars available with or without a driver.

Prestige des Neiges
T +33 (0)4 79 08 00 81

Privilege
T +33 (0)4 79 31 24 24
(chauffeured cars)

RTP Taxi Roger
T +33 (0)4 79 55 31 03
E hotel-athena-brides@wanadoo.fr

Station taxis 1850
T +33 (0)4 79 08 23 46

Toilets

1850
La Croisette (on Place du Tremplin side – check out the great view!). Take the steps down opposite Le Tremplin. Also the ground floor of Le Forum – handy for when you're skiing past.

1650
At the top of the escalator, above the tourist office and opposite the lift pass office.

1550
At road level below the La Grangettes gondola (next to Kikafaim).

La Tania
In the gondola building.

Le Praz
In the gondola building.

Tourist office

Full of useful information including town maps and guides to shopping, bars, restaurants and accommodation.

1850

T +33 (0)4 79 08 00 29
On Place du Tremplin, 9am-7pm daily.

1650

T +33 (0)4 79 08 03 29
Maison de Moriond, open 9am-12pm, 2-7pm (Monday - Friday), 9am-7pm (Saturday-Sunday).

1550

T +33 (0)4 79 08 04 10
Rue des Rois, 9am-12pm, 4-6pm.

Le Praz

T +33 (0)4 79 08 41 60

Underneath the Praz and Forêt gondolas, 8.30am-12pm, 2-5.30pm.

La Tania

T +33 (0)4 79 08 40 40
At the bottom of Folyères near to Le Pub Ski Lodge, 9am-12.30pm, 2.30-7pm.

Trains

> 17.

Weather

Generally you can expect January and February to be colder than March and April. December is less snow-sure but correspondingly cheaper, except around Christmas and New Year. Members of the Ski Club of Great Britain can obtain historical snow reports from the organisation's website (**skiclub.co.uk**).

The following provide current weather forecasts:
maddogski.com – three-day weather forecasts and webcams
meteo.fr/montagne – three day forecasts with snowfall, temperature, wind and avalanche information

Radio Nostalgie Courchevel (93.2fm) and Radio R' Méribel (97.9 and 98.9fm). English weather forecasts between 8-9am.

Mountain forecast
T +33 (0)8 92 68 02 73
Avalanche report
T +33 (0)8 92 68 10 20
– both €0.34 per minute.

Courchevel 1850

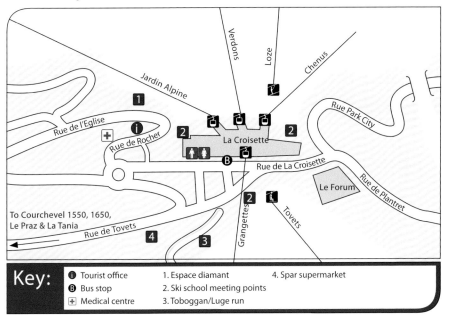

Verdons

Loze

Chenus

Jardin Alpine

Rue de l'Eglise

Rue de Rocher

Rue Park City

La Croisette

Rue de La Croisette

Le Forum

Rue de Plantret

To Courchevel 1550, 1650,
Le Praz & La Tania

Rue de Tovets

Grangettes

Tovets

Key:

- ℹ Tourist office
- Ⓑ Bus stop
- ✚ Medical centre

1. Espace diamant
2. Ski school meeting points
3. Toboggan/Luge run

4. Spar supermarket

Courchevel 1650

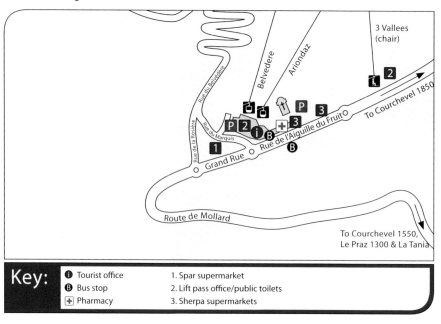

Key:

- **ⓘ** Tourist office
- **Ⓑ** Bus stop
- **✚** Pharmacy

1. Spar supermarket
2. Lift pass office/public toilets
3. Sherpa supermarkets

Courchevel 1550

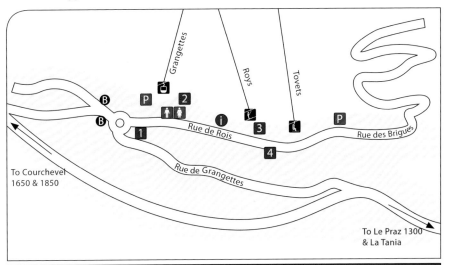

Key:

- ℹ Tourist information & ATM
- 🅱 Bus stop
- 🚻 Public toilets

1. Sherpa
2. Lift pass office
3. Telephones
4. L'Oeil de Boeuf

Courchevel La Tania

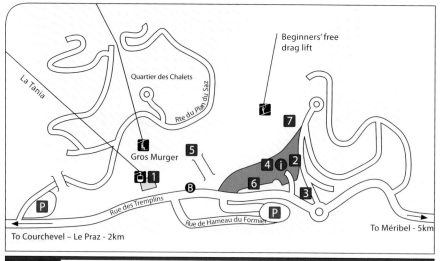

Key:

▨ Main shopping area	1. Lift pass office	4. La Presse (tabac)	6. Public phone
❶ Tourist office	2. ATM	5. Public elevator	7. ESF office and
❷ Bus stop	3. Sherpa	(access to chalets)	meeting point

Courchevel Le Praz

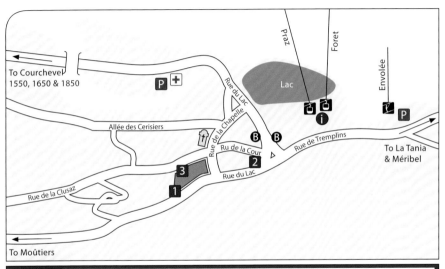

To Courchevel
1550, 1650 & 1850

Allée des Cerisiers

Rue de la Chapelle

Rue du Lac

Lac

Praz

Foret

Envolée

Ru de la Cour

Rue de Tremplins

To La Tania
& Méribel

Rue de la Clusaz

Rue du Lac

To Moûtiers

3
1
2

Key:

■ Main shopping area	**B** Bus stop	1. Post office
i Tourist information – lift pass office, ESF	✚ Medical centre	2. Sherpa
	🛉 Chapel	3. La Presse (tabac)

Index

And finally...
We would like to thank the following people for their help and support: Susie Aust, Matt Bird, Laurence Bourgeois at the Courchevel tourist office, Phillip Blackwell, Carrie Hainge at the Ski Club of Great Britain, Penny Harding, Paddi Hutchins-Clarke, Juliet Johnston, Simon Milton, Erica Meredith Hardy, Louise Moore.

Photo credits
Courchevel tourist office – P144
Stan Berthe – P137
Studio Davolo – P74, 143
Roland Grangier – P127, 128
Divider: About Mad Dog
Jérôme Kélagopian
– P11, 14, 15, 16, 25, 51, 100, 101, 124
Divider: About Courchevel, Food and drink, The list

Pascal Leroy – P7, 48, 60, 69, 134
Divider: Children
Patrick Pachod – P9, 68, 148, 151
Divider: Planning your trip, On the piste
Nicolas Rigaud
Divider: Other things to do
Kate Whittaker – P5, 28, 34, 36. 42, 91
Cover

Do you know something we don't? Jot down your tips and recommendations and let us know about them at info@maddogski.com

Do you know something we don't? Jot down your tips and recommendations and let us know about them at info@maddogski.com

_____

_____

_____

_____

_____

_____

_____

Do you know something we don't? Jot down your tips and recommendations and let us know about them at info@maddogski.com

_____

_____

_____

_____

_____

_____

_____

_____